Single Women

Single Women

AFFIRMING OUR SPIRITUAL JOURNEYS

EDITED BY
Mary O'Brien & Clare Christie

Foreword by
E. Margaret Fulton

BERGIN & GARVEY
Westport, Connecticut
London

Library of Congress Cataloging-in-Publication Data

Single women : affirming our spiritual journeys / edited by Mary
   O'Brien and Clare Christie ; foreword by E. Margaret Fulton.
        p. cm.
      Includes bibliographical references and index.
      ISBN 0–89789–321–2 (HC : alk. paper).—
      ISBN 0–89789–362–X (PB : alk. paper)
      1. Single women—Religious life. I. O'Brien, Mary.
   II. Christie, Clare.
   BL625.7.S56   1993
   248.8′432—dc20   92–39121

British Library Cataloguing in Publication Data is available.

Library of Congress Catalog Card Number: 92–39121
ISBN: 0–89789–321–2
ISBN: 0–89789–362–X (PB)

First published in 1993

Bergin & Garvey, 88 Post Road West, Westport, CT 06881
An imprint of Greenwood Publishing Group, Inc.

Printed in the United States of America

The paper used in this book complies with the
Permanent Paper Standard issued by the National
Information Standards Organization (Z39.48–1984).

10 9 8 7 6 5 4 3 2 1

Contents

Foreword

This volume of essays is a welcome addition to a growing body of literature by women speaking in their own voices and recording different aspects of women's experience. While these writers all demonstrate the common theme that single women remain the most undervalued persons in any culture, by telling their stories they demonstrate not only the tremendous diversity of their experiences of oppression but also the diversity of positive identity as single women. They are finding their real authenticity and rootedness within themselves rather than searching outside themselves for approval and authority, either in a male partner or in the many social and religious institutions of society.

Every type of "single" is represented here: women who chose marriage and then found themselves single because of divorce or widowhood; women who chose the cloister and celibate lives only to be cast out because they did not fit the stereotype of submission to authority; women who remained single by default (no Prince Charming arrived to break the spell of singleness); and women who actually chose being single as their vocation.

The common thread in this diversity of experience is the idea that singleness must be avoided because it is synonymous with loneliness. But as the stories unfold, it becomes clear that loneliness is not limited to being single or to being alone. Many discovered that as they worked through the initial stages of being single, they were far less lonely than when they were isolated in abusive marriages or relationships. The realization that partnerships, marriages, or covenants within religious orders are merely social constructs designed by patriarchal religions as a means of oppressing women becomes the basis of liberation for these women. Some had to seek solitude in order to find themselves; others discovered talents they never knew they had that led to rich professional lives where their newfound empowerment was used to empower others. All seem to have found a new understanding of the solidarity of sisterhood as a basic support for the single woman.

Once free of the shackles of patriarchy, these women become aware of a transforming mission that leaves no time for loneliness but nevertheless demands that they save enough time to be "alone" with their new sense of a cosmic consciousness, a transforming spirit within themselves that keeps them on an integrative or holistic path. This new orientation of the single woman is the very opposite of the egocentric "I-me-my" mentality associated with an anthropomorphic male god. It is rather a true understanding of the cosmic oneness of all in nature.

While the essays contained in this volume provide ample evidence that discrimination against the single woman stems from hierarchical and patriarchal religions, many of the writers in their use of language and in particular their use of the word "God" create images of themselves as mere puppets on a journey that is planned and directed by some external authority with whom there is no interaction. Despite this somewhat negative image of submissive females who suffer trials and tribulations as necessary steps toward strengthening their faith, the more positive image of women taking charge of their own lives with a renewed sense of their unique power dominates. As women find their own voices, one hopes that they will eventually find a new and different language to describe their experiences.

The inconsistencies stemming from language and inadequate use of metaphor in no way deflects from a general awareness that society's obsession and concentration on the centrality of human sexuality has had a diminishing effect on our total human potential. Many of these women believed marriage either to a man or to the church to be the only sanity. By shedding the notion that women can only be fulfilled when in relationship to a man or a male god, these women in fact found their true sanity. Overemphasis on human sexuality prevents people from seeing what their lives and the world can be and leaves them powerless to transform themselves and their societies.

In putting their stories into words, these women have begun a process of openness that can only lead the way for other women of all faiths, single or otherwise, first, to find a richer, deeper form of female spirituality and second, to become more involved in the transformation of society as a whole.

E. Margaret Fulton

Introduction

Mary O'Brien and Clare Christie

Single women's stories can display tremendous courage. They can also be prophetic: they often critique the existing order of things, pointing to ways of creating a more compassionate and just world. It is this vision that inspired *Single Women: Affirming Our Spiritual Journeys*.

In February 1990, we participated in a weekend workshop for single women at the Atlantic Christian Training Centre in Tatamagouche, Nova Scotia. The participants came from a variety of life-styles—ever-single, widowed, and divorced—and our ages ranged from the late twenties to the eighties. Our common bond was the desire to explore ways we as single women could live more fully in a society that places such great emphasis on marriage and narrowly defines family as spouse and children. There were no formal presentations: it was a time of discussion, of sharing, of telling one's own story. Each woman discovered that this was a rare opportunity to search with other women for a deeper meaning to the single life. It was especially a time for each of us to name and define our own unique expressions of singlehood and to be affirmed in our expressions.

We left convinced that the voices of single women need to be heard.

This volume has come to fruition because of the many single women around the world who so willingly responded to our request to write a chapter. Their honesty, insights and enthusiasm have given this work a life of its own, generating an excitement and a vision we did not initially expect.

Many different viewpoints are represented in these pages. Mary O'Brien is in her fifties, divorced with grown children, and prefers to live alone. The coeditor, Clare Christie, is in her forties and ever-single, still fantasizing that an intimate heterosexual relationship could make life even better. As best we can tell, the contributors range in age from the twenties to the seventies; they represent various spiritual traditions and numerous vocations, though a significant number have or have had a strong religious affiliation to their work.

It is to all of our contributors that we dedicate this book, with the hope that in sharing our stories, we all join in spirit with the numerous women among you who are also struggling with and celebrating your singleness. We want our stories to empower you to name your experiences so that you, too, will be affirmed in doing so.

I Stereotypes and Shibboleths: Redefining Singlehood

Living alone as a single woman denotes the most atypical of life-styles, since we live in societies that are dedicated to relationships. In this part, women describe how they have come to terms with the negative definitions and perspectives that are often universally ascribed to singleness.

Mary Ann Cejka provides a powerful opening statement by describing the prejudice against ever-single women and calling for a name for the demon so that it may be disempowered.

"The Single Woman and Sexism" is Beverley Holt's struggle with Christianity's sexism, passing through the depths of pain to spiritual affirmation.

In "Being Poor and Single," Alice Brona presents the reality of women's poverty and her faith, which has sustained her through the experience.

1   A Demon with No Name: Prejudice against Single Women

Mary Ann Cejka

Picture the scene: Two friends from high school, now in their early thirties, are meeting one another for lunch. They study the menus, order, then settle down to visit. They talk for a long while about Ellen's family—about her children's antics at home, her husband's dissatisfaction with his new job, and their plans for adding another room to their home. As the plates are cleared away, Ellen asks Sarah, her single friend, "How about you? Any news?" Sarah proceeds to tell Ellen about her plans for starting her own business, about having joined a local peace coalition, about her hope of spending Christmas with her family. Ellen listens politely but restlessly. Finally, as Sarah pauses to reach for the bill, Ellen interrupts: "But do you have any *news*? You know—I mean, any *men* in your life?"

Many of us who are single have been in Sarah's shoes, making the lonely discovery that our friends do not value events that are very important to us; nothing is really news unless it involves a relationship with a man. The fictional conversation between Ellen and Sarah is but one example of a nonfictional bias in our society against singlehood in women and, by logical extension, against women who are single.

As a student of gender stereotypes, I have come across some interesting research findings. Here is one of them: Strong and diffuse pressures to marry pervade American society, and these pressures have a greater impact upon women than upon men. The fact that 94 percent of all women over thirty in the United States are or have been married attests to the effectiveness of these pressures (Gigy, 322). Like anyone else who deviates from societal norms or expectations, we who constitute the other 6 percent face societal sanctions. Social scientists report that being married is positively and highly valued for women; consistent with this value, single women are viewed less favorably than married women.

In a study entitled "Perceptions of Women: Effects of Employment Status and Marital Status," Claire Etaugh and Barbara Petroski documented a surprisingly negative evaluation of single women among college students. At Bradley University in Peoria, Illinois, Etaugh and Petroski briefly described twelve hypothetical women, half of whom were married and half of whom were not, to 168 male and female students who rated the women on a wide range of personality traits. Etaugh and Petroski found that the students perceived the personality traits more positively if the women being rated were portrayed as married than if they were portrayed as single. Married women were viewed as happier and as more sociable, secure, influential, attractive, and comfortable with others than never-married women. Etaugh and Petroski believe that their findings may reflect "a pervasive, negative stereotype of unmarried women . . . with respect to personality traits" (337).

But many of us who are single do not need to look to scientific studies to know that we often face prejudice—usually subtle, but sometimes blatant—simply because we are single. The prejudice stems from stereotypes based upon the suspicion that something is psychologically wrong with women who never marry.

One such stereotype is that single women are immature. Many single women find that in subtle ways they are less likely to be treated as adults than are their married friends because it is assumed that by not choosing marriage they are avoiding adult responsibilities. Underneath this stereotype lies an understanding of marriage as an adult rite of passage such that those who do not undergo it are regarded as never having passed into adulthood.

Since younger people possess lower social status than adults and women possess lower social status than men, single women are often treated as if they were lower in status than married women. A common expression of the perception that someone is of lower status is to treat that person with greater familiarity than one would treat someone of higher status. For example, single women who are teachers and staff members at colleges and universities may find that students feel freer to address them by their first names or other familiar terms than their married counterparts—an indication that they are regarded as having lower social status than married women.

During my years working in Catholic campus ministry, I learned the power of a name. Certain male students were very uncomfortable with the fact that I, a woman, had been appointed campus minister. One very conservative student, David, even had difficulty looking me in the eye and calling me by my name. Embarrassed to run into me alone on the stairs one afternoon, he greeted me, "Hi there, Blue Eyes!"

On another occasion, one of David's friends had called the local bishop to complain that I had been preaching at Mass, a ministry from which women are excluded by Roman Catholic canon law. Later, when he asked me if I were planning to join him and his friends for pizza that evening, I said that I was. "Good girl!" he gushed.

Such experiences made me aware that my presence as campus minister was a threat to these young men. By addressing me in overfamiliar terms, they were putting me "in my place," that is, letting me know that they did not recognize my status.

If I had been married, they may have been less uncomfortable with my presence, and I doubt that they would have dared to address me as they did, since men are hesitant to transgress what they regard as the territory of another man. If I had been a nun, these conservative students probably would have insisted on calling me "Sister"!

Another expression of the "single woman as immature" stereotype is based upon the syllogism that since women who have not married have not undergone the adult rite of passage that marriage represents, they remain rootless and uncommitted. Often single women find that others are insensitive to their autonomy as adults when, for example, they imply that single women who live away from their families, unlike married women who live with their husbands and children, do not reside at "home." A single woman may feel strongly that the place where she lives and out of which she works is her home, but others assume that her residence is simply a matter of convenience or practicality—surely her real sense of home is with her parents or other relatives. In this way single women receive a message that until they "put down their own roots"—get married—their commitments are to be regarded as trivial and ephemeral, taken on primarily to fill the empty time until they can finally establish themselves in the world of adults through marriage.

Recently I came across a journal entry from my years as a campus minister when I was reflecting upon how the students perceived me:

My students still ask me what I'm going to do when I "grow up." I know they're being facetious when they choose that wording—still, what gives rise to the question? I'm thirty-two years old, hold a four-year professional degree, and I'm doing the work for which I was trained. But they still have a sense that I am not yet doing whatever it is I'm supposed to be doing with my life. In fact, I probably *won't* stay in this ministry forever; but would they be asking me the same question if I were a priest, nun, or someone's wife? Priests, nuns, and wives may go from one job to another and still be regarded as "settled." Despite my credentials, the hours I put in, and the fruits of my labors, I am not regarded as having a profession.

Since single women are viewed as having fewer commitments and responsibilities than married women have, they are also viewed as having "time on their hands." Professional women who are single frequently find that they are expected to do the little "extras" at work—to serve on more committees, volunteer for more overtime, or to give up more holidays and weekends—because they are perceived as having nothing better to do.

It should be noted that single men are also perceived as less mature than married men. However, being single is less detrimental to men's social status than to women's because single women have the additional disadvantage of being female; moreover, women's social status is affected more dramatically by marriage than men's, perhaps because men are less likely than women to be regarded as "unwhole" or "unfulfilled" by not being married. Finally, single professional women are more likely than their male counterparts to be asked to contribute more time at work because women, being of lower social status, are more likely than men to be perceived as approachable.

The lower social status of single women and the fact that we are a minority suggest that we are confronted with stressors unique to our situation. Indeed, one researcher speculated that society's negative image of single women could cause single women to experience detrimental psychological consequences. Comparing a large sample of single and married women in her study "Self-Concept of Single Women," Lynn Gigy found that single women were somewhat more likely than married women to report symptoms indicative of the obsessive-compulsive personality type (330). Other studies indicate that married persons, regardless of sex, are much happier than single persons.

But it would be a mistake to attempt to interpret such results in isolation from a broader social psychological context. Because both men and women who are mentally unstable are unlikely to be selected as marriage partners, they usually remain among the ranks of the single. So it is not the case that most single people are mentally unstable; rather, a few are very unstable, causing the overall rate of psychological disorders among single people to be higher than that among married people.

In his study entitled "The Relationship between Sex Roles, Marital Status, and Mental Illness," Walter Gove compared the incidence of mental illness among men and women, some of whom were married and some of whom were single, and found that whereas married women have higher rates of mental illness than married men, single women tend to be psychologically healthier and considerably happier than single men. Gove suggested that "there is something about the roles [married] women occupy which is difficult and which promotes mental illness. . . . Being married is considerably more advantageous to men than it is to women, while being single is, if anything, slightly more disadvantageous to men than to women" (42–43). Unlike the roles of married women, Gove explained, the roles of single women are not all that different from the roles of single men; additionally, single women are more likely than single men to seek out sources of social and emotional support. Single women, wrote Gove, tend to "form and maintain close interpersonal ties, while single men are more apt to be independent and isolated" (36).

Apparently, the psychological resilience of the majority of single women is due to the fact that while we cherish and maintain close personal ties, we also have a sense of independence and self-determination to a much greater degree than married women. Gigy found that whereas the married women she studied defined themselves in terms of ascribed roles having to do with kinship and household activities, the single women defined themselves in terms of their goals and ideals and their ability to pursue them. The autonomy and self-reliance of single women, suggested Gigy, may in fact be a strong determinant of the choice not to marry (334–335).

Gigy found no significant difference between single and married women in their evaluations of their lives in terms of success. Overall, married women rated themselves as "very happy" and single women as "pretty happy" (329). But single women emerged as having higher self-esteem than married women (331). Single women were more likely than married women to describe themselves as energetic, assertive, and poised, and they were less likely than married women to describe themselves as dull or lazy (332–333).

Some may find it disturbing to learn that single women in Gigy's study were more likely to conceive of themselves in terms of stereotypically masculine characteristics. Such a finding could be construed as evidence that single women have indeed failed at being *women*. (A related assumption is that women who never marry must be lesbians. For the record, 27 percent of single women describe themselves as lesbian, and another 6 percent describe themselves as "predominantly" lesbian [Gigy, 329]. It is important to be aware that they, as well as single women of color, bear the burden of additional societal sanctions and prejudices.)

An alternative to the notion that single women are essentially "unwomanly" is suggested by social role theory, originated by Alice Eagly, eminent gender researcher and professor of psychology at Purdue University. In her book *Sex Differences in Social Behavior: A Social-Role Interpretation*, Eagly explains that certain traits are attributed to people based upon what they are observed to be doing (21). If they are often observed to be carrying out tasks that are perceived as demanding female communal traits—for example, affection, gentleness, sensitivity and helpfulness to others—they are seen as feminine. The same logic applies to those engaged in tasks perceived as demanding male agentic traits, such as daring, courage, ambition and self-confidence; such people are regarded as masculine (22). (The terms "communal" and "agentic" were first employed by David Bakan in his book *The Duality of Human Existence* [14–15].)

In one study, "Gender Stereotypes Stem from the Distribution of Women and Men into Social Roles" (1984), Alice Eagly and Valerie Steffen found that employed people were seen as especially agentic and homemakers as relatively communal, regardless of their sex. Their finding offers evidence that people who carry out a particular activity are perceived to have the traits that their role requires. Similar studies have shown that people are likely to form impressions of another's personality based more upon the role than the sex of the person they are judging. Further, research indicates that men and women in the same occupation are thought to have the same traits.

Hence, if single women are more likely to describe themselves as having stereotypically masculine traits, they are probably basing the description upon their role, not upon their sex. Feminine traits have become associated with the roles of wife and mother. Since we single women are not wives and usually are not mothers and, like men, are more likely than married women to be employed outside the home, we may well use such agentic traits as capableness, adventurousness, activeness, and independence to describe ourselves.

Both Gigy and Gove suggest that the positive, confident, and independent self-concepts of so many single women may account for our ability to withstand society's sanctions against being single. In addition, the fact that we as a group are likely to have continued our education beyond high school has probably aided us in dealing with society's failure to accept and understand us as single women.

Before concluding, I would like to address the specific experience of single Catholic women because I am among them. A central pain of many Catholic single adults is a sense of having fallen through the vocational net. Vocations to marriage, priesthood, and religious life are viewed as normal, understandable, even admirable. People are unlikely to ask

"What's wrong with her?" about a woman who is married, just because she is married, or about a nun, just because she is a nun. Ultimately the greatest temptation that a Catholic single—or perhaps anyone who is single—must face is that of believing that because she does not have a spouse or because she lacks the title and status of a priest or vowed religious, she is therefore worthless, unloved and unlovable, fatally flawed in some way that the rest of the world knows but does not want to tell her. I have called such thoughts a temptation, and the word *temptation* is carefully chosen. Temptation is the lobbying effort of illusion, and the illusion is born of the societal sanctions against women who dare to live full, happy, and creative lives without being attached to men.

Some years ago, while I was facilitating a singles' discussion group at Catholic Family Services, one woman shared how she had gradually come to realize that her marital status was irrelevant to her value as a human being:

If I didn't know that I am a treasure—even if an unclaimed treasure; that I am not here by accident; that simply by being, I am connected with all that is in a way that transcends any volitional commitment I could make; that the divine knows and cherishes my beauty; then I would forever be trying to reshape myself into someone who deserves love (as if love were deservable). I've known what it's like to be trapped in "if onlys": if only I had thinner thighs, a darker tan, or longer hair, if only I were a more interesting person, if only I didn't talk so much, if only I were less intelligent so that I could be beaten at Scrabble—in other words, if only I weren't *me*, then I'd be lovable. But living in the "if onlys" makes us bow to the illusion that society continues to uphold—i.e., that we really would be much better off married—and as long as we are capitulating to an illusion, we cannot expect to be at peace.

The theologian Michael Downey (1986) has written that grace is to be found "between the cracks" of society and its institutions (including its religious institutions). The life-giving activity of the divine (or grace) usually emerges where it is least expected:

We must look in different places, to the cracks and the dregs, to the fringes and the margins, to the "rents in the veil." By looking to the edges and the cracks, we glimpse that it is there that the quest for a truly human life continues in our terrible age, an age in the history of humanity that seems hopelessly bent on self-destruction. (119)

The fact that we who are ever-single women make up a mere 6 percent of all women defines us as statistically marginal and thus qualifies us uniquely as bearers of the grace that will bring healing and salvation to our ravaged planet.

It may be difficult, however, for others, particularly those who are the least marginalized, to recognize our grace-bearing vocation. Ugly names for single women are only gradually being dispelled from conventional vocabulary. Not so very long ago, we would have been referred to as spinsters and old maids—words that conjure up images of dour, inflexible aunties who wear homely clothing, fill their lonely hours with trivial chores, and grow old before their time.

In fact, people are not sure *what* to call us—and thus resort to defining us negatively, as in "unmarried" women. I heard a priest use yet another appellation: I had been asked by a Catholic television broadcasting station to appear as a member of a panel for a program called "The Single Life." Two of us on the pánel were single women, and the third was a parish priest, apparently a "regular" on the series. He chatted with us before the filming began, probably to put us at ease, asking us what it was like to be bachelorettes. Bachelorettes? I felt as if I were appearing on a game show! When I told him that I would rather be referred to as a single woman, he looked at me as if I were dangerous. During the actual filming of the panel discussion, he was careful to do most of the talking.

Perhaps the reason why people are still not sure what to call us is that, despite the fact that the status of single women has improved markedly over the last few decades, the negative stereotypes of single women have proven to be as resilient as we ourselves. The stereotypes feed and are fed by a pervasive prejudice against women who do not marry. But as yet there exists no name for this prejudice.

Other forms of prejudice have names. Words such as *racism, sexism, heterosexism,* and *clericalism* are widely recognized and understood today. We can point to each and say, "This is wrong, it hurts people, it must be changed." But there is no word for prejudice against single people or in particular against single women, whose marital status is considered a more serious problem than that of single men.

The desert mothers and fathers, that is, those Christians of the fourth century who fled to the desert to live as hermits when the church began to make serious compromises with the Roman Empire, had a rule about doing battle with demons: *name* the offending demon. Once the demon is named, its power to harm is seriously compromised. We who do battle with the demon of prejudice against single women need to name this demon.

Perhaps the naming will not be easy. Perhaps we will need to do a lot of talking, praying, and studying together before we find a name for the demon that offends us. We might have to try piloting a few names like "maritalism" (but it doesn't communicate that single *women* bear the brunt of this demon) or "wife-ism" (but it's an awkward construction) until the right name presents itself. But the demon must be named or it will continue to be invisible to all but those of us whom it afflicts.

The demon won't disappear once it is named, but we will have an important new handle on it. We can learn how not to succumb to it. We can educate others about it and work toward transforming the structures that keep it alive. People will find it harder to say, "You're imagining that," or "That isn't really happening," when "that" has a name.

Prejudice against single women is real. We experience it in our relationships, in our work, and through the media. Yet we have remained silent about it, perhaps because many of us are already engaged in working against myriad other forms of prejudice. As women, after all, we have been socialized to put the needs of others before our own, to cooperate with the expectations of patriarchal society and patriarchal church. Most of us carry many responsibilities, but as single women, we are also responsible for one another. It is now time for us to rise to the challenge of naming the demon of prejudice against us.

2 The Single Woman and Sexism: One Woman's Struggle with Christianity's Sexism

Beverley Holt

> The new wave of feminism desperately needs to be not only many faceted but cosmic and ultimately religious in its vision.
>
> Mary Daly, *Beyond God the Father*, 29

> The things which happened to me have actually turned out for the furtherance of the Gospel.
>
> Philippians 1:2

"For a year now the adults of our church have been divided into house groups for midweek Bible studies. It's been a good idea."

The person explaining this to me was a woman I knew well. I have been part of her family often in my sixteen years of traveling ministry as New Zealand's National Baptist Youth Director. Her voice had that tinge of confidentiality that alerted me to listen carefully.

"I gave each leader," she said, "every one of them a caring man, the opportunity to let me know who does not fit into his group and [said] I would rearrange the groupings." She waved a piece of paper in despair. "The name of every widow in the scheme has been given to me! They are wonderful women, every one of them. Stalwarts of the church, saints!"

I began to talk about being single in our "family"-oriented churches, but it seemed as though there had to be more to it than that. I had been appointed as National Youth Director at the beginning of the 1970s. It was a wonderful time to enter youth ministry—there was so much to do after the upheavals of the 1960s. But for the first three years it was a rare minister who gave me more than five minutes of his pulpit time to speak to the congregation. When I was given the chance I made sure the sermon wasn't just good—it was the best!

Unfortunately a side effect of doing well publicly, especially at the large Annual Assemblies, was the inevitable written letter of introduction from a despairing bachelor who had confirmation from God that I met all the requirements he needed in a wife. I remember feeling like well-displayed merchandise. The macho male on our rugged West Coast, however, always found an excuse for being unexpectedly called away whenever I made the eight-hour trek over the Southern Alps to visit his youth group. I never knew if this was out of shame at his youth work or fear of being visited by an unmarried woman. Both had been hinted at.

Actually, the male cynics I encountered in those early years were hard to take. "I've been teaching Bible class for nine years—what does she think she can teach me?" was the message relayed indirectly to me from more than one male. But after three tough years I sensed I was being accepted and respected as a youth worker. For one thing, I had the backing of the Christian education director and the general superintendent of the denomination, who, as my mentor, enabled me to enter denominational ministry in the first place and who, before he moved back into pastoral ministry, announced to the Union Council, "Ladies and gentlemen, our youth work has been saved."

Because of the constant traveling and the evening and weekend work involved, it was a ministry that I believe could only have been done by a single person, and probably only by a single woman. For nine years, for instance, I had no base or office. Everything I needed for work and living was in my car. While I worked in a particular church, at the members' invitation, I lived in their homes. I became part of their families; I was given a sense of belonging to their churches. I grew to care for them deeply. My particular gift was vision. I could visit the most unpromising youth group and see all its possibilities. And because I was prepared to live on the job, it did not take long as I worked alongside leaders, churches, and parents before the possibilities began to be realized.

My greatest joy was to develop the potential within people. Ordinary ministers became guest speakers at youth gatherings of hundreds or even thousands of young people; housewives became outstanding youth pastors; teenagers became song leaders and group leaders; they learned clowning, puppetry, and creative dance and shared their faith in hospitals, prisons, and in almost all our surrounding Asian countries. Full musical productions, creative church worship services, and overseas mission trips became possible for all youth groups, whether they numbered 120 or 12, no matter how talented or "ordinary" they thought they were! Through New Zealand–wide gatherings, a sense of unity and national identity developed. Best of all, competitive youth groups became places of acceptance and nurture. Leaders and young people alike began to see themselves as having value, talents, and courage. I received a lot of love and appreciation in return.

How was it that my name was now on a list of the "unwanted"?

What I had seen happening to widows in that Wellington church had begun to happen to me! My fourteen years of stalwart service seemed to be forgotten, to become invisible, just as it had when the centenary history of the denomination and the fortieth anniversary history of my home church were written, omitting my theological degree, my length of ministry, and my positive achievements.

And now I was on trial in front of twelve men who saw themselves as judge and jury. Some had hardly been to a Youth Department board meeting before, but they were not about to miss this one! After all, they were the ones who had taken the unprecedented step of contacting the new general superintendent to express their concern at my "manner." "I'm told you are ill," the general superintendent informed me when he rang up on that fated Monday morning. I had laughed at first, wondering how such a rumor had begun, but when I heard who had been the one to contact him and found that my protestations were being taken as "obvious signs" of an illness, I knew this was serious.

The board member who "blew the whistle" on me had joined us at the beginning of that year at our biannual youth gathering. We were delighted to have him there and thought nothing of his sitting up into the small hours of the morning with a troubled youth leader who was also present at the gathering, listening to her story. When another board member discovered the continuing indiscretion between this young woman and the "caring" board member many months later, the situation was discussed privately between these two male board members, was forgiven and forgotten. (Except that the young woman was suspended from her youth ministry for six months and, eventually, as time has shown, forever. The man, who kept pestering the young woman for at least another three years, emerged free of any blame or consequences and is happily and fully involved with the church. The "punished" young woman still can't face the "Christianity" that could be so unjust.)

These happened to be the same two men who had reported my "indisposition" to the general superintendent without any private discussion with me. Why? Had I not tried every way I knew of helping the board to work? I had spoken with business consultants who alerted me to the importance of meeting format, seating arrangements, and preparation of board papers. I always saw that a full meal was served before meetings—it was hard work. Despite this, negativity had often been the dominant experience for me in board meetings.

It is true that I had had one board chairman several years earlier who not only offered constructive ideas but who popped in at least weekly to see how things were going. Baptist youth ministry had flourished with such teamwork. The beginnings of the national magazine and the overseas mission trips were also spearheaded by board members.

I had no illusions. Some people are great at working in a team, but a board system where people get themselves elected favors the ambitious and those craving power rather than those able to serve.

In fact, in spite of working predominantly with men and having the support of some deeply caring men, I now wonder if I had ever been really accepted as a colleague in this male-oriented denominational ministry? A familiar worry for women in similar circumstances, I now hear.

It is my experience that women who don't "belong" to a man are not seen as women or are seen, subconsciously of course, as belonging to all men. An older woman in youth ministry, recognizing my predicament, spoke earnestly to me about this, for she well knew she had survived mainly because she was seen as without gender. If these attitudes had become visible earlier, I could have faced them and challenged such a system, but in my naivete, I had no idea that the sin of sexism, with its cruel domination system researched and clearly outlined by the women's movement, is also woven into the very fabric of the Christian faith.

For thirteen years I had conformed to white male system values and procedures, but I had failed in the second requirement; as researcher and author Dr. Anne Wilson Schaef warns, "We must never threaten the men with or for whom we work" (1985, 41).

There I was, therefore, sitting for seven hours at that board table with an all-male board, hearing accusations that were trivia from those who were supposed to be colleagues!

I was not communicating enough detail.

I was developing the work too fast.

It was all summed up by the general superintendent: "You haven't been able to keep everybody happy, Beverley, and that is what ministry is all about." I murmured that I wasn't sure whether Jesus had done so well on that criteria, either!

Later, when the general superintendent was asking the denomination to be understanding of the changes largely initiated by him, he wrote the poignant words, "The Christian church, of all communities, ought to be one where people are allowed to grow, to make mistakes, and to try again in an atmosphere of encouragement and affirmation."

I was staggered. I had experienced no atmosphere of encouragement and affirmation, no acceptance that people learn from mistakes, no allowance for growth. Indeed, training, supervision, or personal development was never even considered by the authorities. All I ever heard was either, "Go back to being the up-front youth leader doing everything yourself and thereby ensuring it is done well," or the remedy used in *Alice in Wonderland* for any failure, "Off with her head!" Both dictates attacked my integrity, as they seemed a betrayal of my sense of God's call on my life.

At 2:30 A.M. that November night, my ordeal around the board table was over, I thought. But as my daily Bible readings led me through the last seven chapters of Mark's Gospel, I began to sense that I was grappling with something much bigger and more complex than I had realized before. It took three years to clarify and to extricate myself from the struggle with the sin of sexism. Often the pain during this time was such that I feared that I would not live to see it through. And in a way I was right, for it was going to be the death of many of my beliefs and much of myself.

I realize now that that traumatic board meeting opened my eyes. It also opened my mouth! I found myself expressing my inner pain with the words, "I feel verbally raped." That was the first outraged awareness that broke free from my forty-year contribution to the generations of women's silence. The silence during which single women missionaries were sent home to New Zealand without a second chance or even a warning that it was being considered as a "remedy." The silence of the ordained women who, over the years, have drifted away from Baptist church pastoral work. All those I know of have been single women, have been good if not outstanding at their work, and have faded from the scene in total silence.

The private trauma, triggered into consciousness by my board experience and its consequences, was a childhood sexual abuse that kindly church and family authorities had said was "never to be mentioned again." The child at the time had obediently forgotten. It wasn't until this second experience of being violated, now by a "Christian" group of men, that the first forgotten experience with another "nice" man, was hooked and dragged to the surface. The grief was overwhelming, for, as well as having to deal with the abuse itself, the abuse experience had formed itself into a set of beliefs I had unconsciously lived by, beliefs reinforced by the male orientation of my beloved Christianity. I began to see how sexual harassment and abuse, reinforced by male-dominated Christianity, has moulded many women, from the way they walk, talk and dress even to their right to live.

However, the most important choice taken from me by this combination of sexual abuse and sexist Christianity was that of marriage. The unconscious but overwhelming need for safety had robbed me of the choice. I've enjoyed being single. I've delighted in the freedom and the opportunities it has brought for ministry and living. I believe that singleness is a great life-style. I am angry, though, at being cheated out of the inner freedom to choose. The tragedy, for me, was the loss of motherhood. I found a substitute by nurturing hundreds of young people over the years. Youth ministry is like that. But it's the awesome, godlike creation of a new life during pregnancy, the physical birthing and the suckling of the infant from within one's own body that draws me to motherhood. In biological motherhood I recognize much of the specialness of being a woman. It's a privilege denied me, initially by sexual abuse, but denied again and again by each experience of verbal, emotional, and spiritual abuse from sexism.

Trying to play safe by staying single hadn't worked, either. The pain of betrayal came from the men who for over fifteen years had been brothers to me. I called the one who had finally sealed my fate with officials because of what he had heard from others. I reminded him of how I had believed in him fifteen years earlier when his youth ministry was in tatters, that since then I had often stayed in his home, been a friend to his wife and children and that we had worked together on many projects as colleagues. "Why would you believe that sort of rumor without first checking it out with me?" It hadn't occurred to him! In the following three years, I came to the painful realization that single womanhood meant unprotected womanhood. And also that competent, respected, single women are a threat to many men, especially within the Christian church, which is perhaps perceived by them as their last hope for sexist domination. There seemed to be a lot of time and energy available for proving that women in general, and Bev in particular, "didn't have what it takes."

Not belonging to a man had a second handicap. If there had been a husband, the men could have gone to him, man to man, and talked about the difficulties they were experiencing with me. Somehow that would have concluded the matter. I've seen that happen again and again, when married women "err." As a single woman, I had no one for them to talk to, as they would not bring their complaints to me face-to-face.

I even asked for the protection of an ombudsman (an impartial person) to help both the hierarchy and myself through the rough waters that threatened us both—me through loss of ministry and reputation, them through the possible public exposure of their immoral actions and decisions. All denominational staff agreed that such an appointment was important, as did the new executive council. I was assured twice that such an appointment was being made. It still has not been. Male solidarity? Or institutional evil? No one inquires.

That's where the heaviest pain lies. Sexism and injustice are bad enough, but to have thousands of church members allowing this to continue year after year is shattering. God, is this how it has to be?

At the climax in June 1987, the executive presented me with a poorly typed, eight-paragraph document expressing the board's vote of confidence in the board member whose history was showing repeated sexual abuse of women. The document showed the board's lack of confidence in me, lack of concern for me, or perhaps just its lack of humanity toward me by stating that I was to submit to his leadership.

This vote of no confidence raised another difficulty. I agreed with them! It was as though I had external circumstances clobbering me from without, but also there was a sympathetic internal response. So many fine men could not be wrong. "It must be as they say. Are they not pastors?" I was inches away from suicide. The external trauma in my life had caused inner trauma. The subconscious death wish I had mastered and suppressed all my life was now fully activated. It was the only honorable way out. I had no right to live, that was obvious. I remember that weekend crisis vividly. By night I walked the beach, wrapped in the darkness. My numbed consciousness seemed aware only of the possible finality in those Tasman Ocean breakers. By day I sat in a rocking chair, bewildered, totally alone. The pain became so extreme that twice I actually lost consciousness and found myself on the floor. I knew something was dying, and I wept bitterly at the price I had paid for being, for so long, the lone, single and thereby unprotected woman in a church hierarchical institution as a denominational staff member.

And yet they had been wonderful years of ministry for me. Numbers trebled in Bible classes and youth groups. Love, acceptance, and support began to replace competitiveness and teasing. The introduction of creative ministries moved "average" young people out of the pews and made them exciting participants in the wider life of the church.

We helped youth leaders develop their youth group structure so as to encourage the spiritual and personal growth of every young person. Adventure was one of our big tools. We encouraged camping and community living, right through to developing a five-month program of picking fruit in orchards in Nelson and Central Otago. Whole towns were influenced by the exuberance of the youths' Christian witness.

All my energies had been going into ministry. I knew how to work all night when necessary. My ministerial day off during those last seven years was for keeping my house, clothes, and garden in order. When the body complained, I knew what sort of vitamins to add to my diet.

Being a single person allowed me to do this. But often it came from the pressure of not having the excuse of the married of "needing to be home for the family." I hear this sense of pressure often now from single women.

I had little understanding of how to channel my Christian commitment inward. I had been well taught not to consider self. "Not I but Christ" had been ingrained through hymns, sermons, and years of practice. But my best was not considered good enough.

At first I was too bewildered by the crumbling of the fabric of my life to take active steps toward recovery. It was at this point that sisterhood began for me. "Enough was enough," a number of women said. They joined the board. Each month five strong, intelligent women lined up on one side of the board table and faced their male opposition. It was amazing and horrible to watch. The married women knew how to "handle" the men; the single women treated them as adults and were not found "comfortable" by the men. As soon as I was safe, all these women left the board. Not one of these capable women is now on a denominational board.

Life began to seep back into me as a result of an Anglican woman's invitation to Sing and Dance the Music of the Mystics. At this stage of my life, anyone less inclined toward singing and dancing than myself would have been hard to find, and I had no idea what was meant by "Mystics," except they hadn't hurt me yet. Each Friday night for two hours this zombie, functioning on will power, was enveloped in much-needed acceptance, harmony, gentleness, and love. The resurrection that seemed never possible gradually emerged. The newness was scary but increasingly beautiful.

Just then, my work led me to discover and apply the basics of understanding personalities using the Myers-Briggs Type Indicator, and a new world began to reveal itself to me. It was a world that understood differences and actually affirmed them. I was an INFJ in Myers-Briggs terms, along with 1 percent of the population, a beautiful but fragile type, they said. As I read my profile and that of my male counterparts, I kept exclaiming, "No wonder! Of course! That's it!"

My experience and observation now echo the sentiments of author Mary Daly who, in the book *Beyond God the Father*, wrote:

Women and men inhabit different worlds. Even though these are profoundly related . . . there is a wall that is visible to those who almost have managed to achieve genuine interplanetary communication with the opposite sex. The prerequisite for this achievement is . . . discovery of the lost self. Half a person can never really meet the objectified other half. (171)

I grieve at our denomination's continued suspicion of personal development and its refusal, at my final assembly in 1989, to deliberately move toward a balance of men and women in denominational structures. I do recognize, however, that the inclusion of women into the institutional hierarchy will have no effect on our church life unless the hierarchy is radically transformed by it.

I think of the young women I encouraged into a church in which, I realize now, they will experience spiritual and emotional abuse. While congregations are exhorted to sing of a military God who fights and conquers, I grieve for the hidden, unrecognized, discounted pain of generations of women and weep for the women who have yet to experience this travesty of Christianity. For, although I hear lip service, I see no depth of change coming into the system.

My spiritual hell began when my own abused past and those of countless other women came into focus and I asked bitterly, "Where was God when this was happening?" I can never pretend now that good intentions are adequate for male pastors trying to minister to women.

"We are taught," Dr. Wilson Schaef writes, "that we will be all right if we can only attach ourselves to an innately superior being, a man, who will then intercede for us" (1985, 37). When I read her book, *Women's Reality*, I wondered if Dr. Wilson Schaef had been monitoring my situation.

As a single woman I had indeed worked from that unconscious belief that I needed verification from a male, be he father, pastor, or boss. They had been the significant people with much power over me.

After my years within aggressive, male-oriented theology, I was discovering that the Mystics, whose music I sing, and the women from whom I was experiencing sisterhood seemed to know and to experience the tender gentleness of a nurturing, mothering God who empowers rather than controls. They highlighted the neglected Biblical perspective of a mother/father God (for example, El Shaddai is defined in the Scofield Bible as El = masculine, Shaddai = feminine, from the Hebrew root word for woman's breast). These new words, and still too often, new concepts, I find very healing and supportive of women. They have been life to me.

I began attending women's worship and was amazed that here were adults doing the sort of beautiful, creative things I had been doing within youth groups, regarded as immature and unnecessary by many within the church. The truth dawned on me that these gentle, creative rituals are powerful and certainly more appropriate for women's spiritual nourishment than the all-too-often weekly sermon of guilt with its exhortation to try harder. Women seemed free and alive in these new environments—and safe. ·

Unknown to me, God was laying the basis of my future life and ministry. Within weeks of my "farewell" from denominational ministry, women were finding their way to my home, wanting company as they too walked the beach, pouring out their longing for a God who makes sense to them and expressing their need for a faith that gently and fully accepts, embraces, and transforms their life experiences. There is no turning back for me. I never want to return to the atmosphere of suspicion and fear, created by too many Christian groups, toward those who are different or who believe differently.

My resurrection insists on bringing a transformed Being into the universe, not just the resuscitated one I expected. Here I am. New. Vulnerable. Unfamiliar to myself. Aware that on this new shore are thousands of other New Zealand women, mainly unaware of each other but all on this same journey. The New Zealand Baptist Denomination loses an average of 1,559 members each year, only 200 to 250 of these through deaths. I wonder how many of the remaining 1,309 are women? How many are single women? How many blame themselves?

I long to see change within the Christian church. Consequently, I am deliberately linking with people who are prepared to be there for each other in any experience of injustice or pain, no matter whose fault. I want to remain part of the New Zealand Baptist family, but I am not willing to be an active part of a hierarchical, sexist system that does not plan to change and yet causes so much damage.

More and more, I discover women and men who feel a similar concern and want to discover whether transformation of the church is possible or we should simply look for another. One group of us meets fortnightly. And because of our pain within the church, we work at our love and acceptance of each other until it is unconditional and inclusive. It is explicitly understood that wherever a person is in the spiritual journey, that's fine for them. The freedom and encouragement to spiritually explore or be "stuck" is given with understanding and wisdom. Permission to trust our own inner promptings is pivotal. We encourage each other to learn wherever possible and to bring back our riches for the benefit of all.

After what we have experienced, we see no place for a hierarchy in our growing ministry of spiritual direction and retreats nor in our wider Spirituality Network. Leadership is taken up as needs and vision arise by those keen and ready for it. Pastoral care is based on each of us taking responsibility for being aware of our own needs and doing whatever we need to do to have those needs met. False rescuing, which leaves people unskilled except in asking the obliging St. George to ride on in and deal with their unfaced dragon, is taboo. We have suffered too much from the cowardice of the unskilled and the clumsiness of the St. Georges.

Consequently, we actively and deliberately encourage personal growth toward wholeness: living in the present, being flexible and non-judgmental, open and warm in expressing oneself, and capable of intimacy. God talk has decreased. God awareness has increased. Theological beliefs held for years are changing radically in emphasis and experience but, surprisingly, not in essence.

I see single women as being the catalyst for these changes. Married women do not normally have the advantage that we have in that we are unprotected from and therefore exposed to the dynamics of life. We are free to make changes and to explore our True Selves without causing our male partners to be ridiculed by the patriarchal system as either being wimps or traitors.

I believe that just as Jesus Christ chose the single life to fulfill his ministry of transformation, single women today have a wonderful and unique opportunity to be healers of our world.

3   Being Poor and Single

Alice Brona

From 1980 to 1990 I was both poor and single. When my marriage ended I became a statistic: divorced, unemployed. I had heard about women and poverty, but I didn't think it could happen to me. When the lawyer I consulted told me that unless I asked for support I'd be living on welfare in public housing, I dropped him. I didn't want to consider the possibility.

Being poor is no fun. People are not nice to the poor. I find the indignity of it incredible, the total loss of privacy. The do-gooders' readiness to blame and the red tape of social agencies make begging mandatory.

From 1980 to 1985 I lived well under the poverty line on my "division of family assets" and money that my father left me. I worked fee-for-service at health education and free-lance writing. When I looked for a full-time job I didn't find one. So I went back to school, relying on student loans and family benefits.

In Women's Studies, I remember the teacher saying, "Society doesn't approve of divorced women and so society punishes them." I tried to block that out. I also learned that people will stop at nothing to protect their own interests and that the poor economy was making people very cautious. I read a study done by the Status of Women that said that besides coping with the hardships of poverty, women spend a lot of energy coping with the care givers. It's not true, I thought. But it is true.

I hear the remarks that stereotype poor women. "When will she come to her senses? If she really wanted a job, she'd get one. She'll just have to take what she can get and not be so fussy. Don't you get sick of people who are always asking for handouts? She should never have left him. Better find a husband before it's too late." That's the hardest part of being poor: being labeled, being judged.

I learned from my mother to rely on divine Providence. God will provide. Whatever you need will be given to you. I believe it, I count on it, and again and again I am saved by faith. Because I receive divine assistance, I am one of the invisible poor.

The other hard part of being poor is not being believed. Poor people are supposed to be silent as well as invisible. When they do talk, no one wants to hear, no one wants to believe.

POOR AND SINGLE

I avoided writing this chapter. I missed the first submission deadline without much disappointment. Maybe I even felt a little relief at being let off the hook. But when I think about this as an opportunity for woman's voice to be heard, I must write.

One of the most painful aspects of poverty is a loss of privacy. Wherever you go for medical, social, legal, or educational services, there are endless forms to fill out requiring personal information that you would hesitate to give your best friend. I hate this loss of privacy, as I was raised at a time when privacy was at the top of the list of values we held dear. With this loss of privacy comes a loss of respect and dignity. It places you in a vulnerable position, open to abuse by those who offer "services." I call this legal "battering," and there's more of it going on than we are willing to admit.

In Women's Studies and feminist writing we are told that the personal is political. If it's happening to me, I can be sure that it's happening to others as well. Feminists say that telling the truth is a subversive act. Speaking out brings reprisals. Most people feel uncomfortable and threatened by it. Especially in these tough economic times, people are conservative, cautious, nervous, insecure, afraid of upsetting the status quo. They prefer to hang on by their fingernails to whatever they've got—better than being a bag lady! One woman said, "I'd rather be rich and miserable than poor and miserable."

So we do tell our stories. We name our reality in the hope of transforming it. If enough women say, "This is what is happening to me, I don't like it, it hurts, and I'm not taking it anymore," there will be a shift. Women make up more than 50 per cent of the population, so if we all say "No, we're not doing it that way any more," it will make a difference in society.

To those people complaining about paying taxes, the recession, and the country's deficit because of "those people" who stay at home collecting Family Benefits, to those who ask "Why aren't they out working?" I can answer. As a single parent, I was eligible for a program to assist reentry to the work force. In 1988 these jobs were full-time, entry-level positions with nonprofit organizations. They paid $16,000 plus benefits for one year. The Ministry of Community and Social Services sent you out as an applicant and if hired, "Com. Soc." would pay the salary for one year, after which time the employer could hire you, or at least you would be more employable when applying for another position. It was a good program. But there were not enough of these positions. Over half a million people (522,800 in July 1988) benefit from social assistance in Ontario. Aside from the fact that getting one of these jobs would have been similar to winning the lottery, here are some of the reasons why I wasn't hired. I was told, "There must be some mistake; this is an entry-level position. You are overqualified." In some instances I had more education than the senior person. They didn't hire me because their other staff wasn't getting paid that well. The unions wouldn't let them create a new position without offering it to the workers with seniority. Some agencies routinely do their staffing through such funding and already had a person waiting for the job when they applied for the program. They didn't even call for interviews. Such inbreeding is common. By 1990, the provincial reentry jobs were paying less, $8 per hour, and more were part-time, reflecting what was happening in the rest of society.

Employers today want community college graduates working part-time for low wages with no benefits and no job security. Many agencies depend on staffing through high school and community college co-op education programs. An increasing trend of part-time, minimum-wage work done by high school students has cut deeply into available jobs among the old standbys of restaurant work and department store clerks. In plain English, there are very few real jobs out there.

The social control of women continues today by keeping them financially dependent. Many women work in nonpaying jobs. They are not paid a salary but have to generate enough money to pay themselves. The company gets paid first, and the woman gets paid if there's any money left over. Women are drawn into selling real estate, life insurance, and products such as cosmetics, jewelery, Tupperware, Amway, erotica, and others with the promise of making good money in their spare time. In fact, most women are left disappointed, and some are left out of pocket and with a closet full of products that they couldn't unload.

I had a similar "nonjob" offer. Before marriage I worked in a medical clinic as a public health nurse and received a good salary plus benefits. When I applied for what I thought was a similar job, the clinic was not going to pay me. In fact they wanted to charge me rent for office space, and I would have had to bill the patients for health counseling. This was a clinic where doctors were making $400,000 per year. I call that nerve! In that clinic, a doctor's assistant (not a nurse) got paid minimum wage. The joke at this place was "We hire monkeys here, because we pay them peanuts."

In an attempt to gain independence, more women are starting small businesses. At first they are lucky if they break even. They can rarely expect to draw a salary for the first couple of years. It's very risky and should only be undertaken with financial backing and good, honest consulting services.

Like many other recycled housewives, I went back to school. I studied equal opportunity management, thinking that since it was a new area, "they" would be crying for people who had that know-how. When I went job hunting I met with ignorance: those who thought that because they accept applications from women and men, they were already equal opportunity employers or those who didn't want to hear the words "employment equity" and were just hoping it would go away. In fact, at a feminist employment counseling agency, my counselor told me not to even mention that I had studied equal opportunity management. "It's like waving a red flag in front of a bull," she said.

I had no way of getting into a human resources department because I lacked five years experience in personnel work and because I did not have a certificate. I have yet to meet someone with the qualifications they are asking for. Programs of study are just being set up in this city. They are lengthy, offering only one or two courses per year. And you must already be employed in human resources before they accept you into the study program: a catch-22.

People in academia might wonder what methods of escape women have found for themselves. Five years ago some friends and I would joke that we were scheming up devious plans to get rich such as a nursing home for rich old folks with no relatives. The home would have well-polished waxed floors. Anything would be preferable to poverty. One friend with uncommon foresight said, "I've been saving for my divorce for ten years—now I'm rich!" My favorite equal opportunity joke came from Erica Ritter, who said it's not fair that women never get invited to be in organized crime.

I no longer think these jokes are funny. Many women have discovered that you can't live without money and have tried desperately to save face by the lure of quick cash: jobs as strippers, pornography models, escorts, hookers, drug dealers, couriers (more recently called "mules") who travel and carry drugs or money from one place to another. Prostitution used to be called "a fate worse than death." I remember the old classic World War

II movie *Victoria Stations* was on that theme. In today's society of greed and profit, receiving Family Benefits is a fate worse than death, and women who are desperate financially endure humiliation and exploitation to avoid it. At best it is precarious, as eligibility stops if the chilren go to live with their father. When this happens and the payments stop, you have to apply all over again as a new case to the welfare department or become a bag lady, another homeless person. It's humiliating: you feel like a beggar.

In social justice courses you learn that people have a right to home ownership and a right to a job. Society doesn't recognize these rights. You start to feel like you have no rights at all . . . no right to exist. You walk around feeling guilty. A friend who was job hunting took her two pre-schoolers to day care in the morning and then stopped at the public library to use the washroom and to put on some makeup. The security guard told her that he was watching her. I feel like a criminal for riding my bicycle on the sidewalk, but it's preferable to being hit by a car. I often have to put items back when I get to the checkout at the supermarket: I have more items than money. Poverty is a feeling of being worn down and being kept down. Being a student helps the morale and is a preferable label to being unemployed.

It takes all my time and energy coping, keeping my head above water, treading water lest I be drowned in a sea of papers. The poor are deluged with forms to fill out, papers to be signed, letters from agencies, lawyers, collection companies, legal jargon, red tape, bureaucratic mess-ups. It isn't easy to sort through the maze. How do people less educated manage? For example, I was robbed by a bank. Because of their mistake, I was dealing with seven individuals in seven different offices over student loans. I had to do it all myself. I have no secretary. I am one individual dealing with hundreds of minions. For another example, I filed a Human Rights complaint because I was not given an equal opportunity for a job I applied for. I had to do all my own paperwork, writing, phoning, going into the office, complaining to another office that they were too slow. It took a year to be told that the complaint was not under the jurisdiction of Human Rights. I was discriminated against not because of age but because I do not have a master's degree. A master's degree is not a bona fide occupational qualification to work with the healthy elderly in their own homes! Now will it take another year for the Employment Equity Commission to deal with it? These offices that supposedly exist to help people are a hassle and a headache. They wear you down.

When people ask what I do, I say I do my best, but it certainly feels like I'm just treading water. In the meantime I've also been sorting through the maze of Canada Pension credits, custody, access, child support, a search for affordable housing, university courses, part-time work, job hunting, the ombudsman's office, family matters, poverty, and illness. It's like juggling and walking a tightrope at the same time. Imagine trying to keep six balls in the air and living a life at the same time. It can't be done!

The ultimate insult is when the service providers tell you the delay is because they are so busy and don't have enough staff. "Well, why don't you hire me?" I ask. I have been labeled a difficult person. I am an overserviced person. Why don't they give us jobs instead of medical care and social workers? We need citizen's advocates who go to offices with us, who cosign letters with us to provide some back-up support, if only to be a witness to what goes on.

Women living in poverty have no real hope that things will get any better. This has been documented, and studies refer to the downward spiral in their standard of living. When I hear of university professors who get large research grants in addition to their salaries to study women in poverty, I think of how much better spent the money would be if $20,000 of it was given to even one poor woman to get her out of poverty for one year.

The frustration of being poor and unemployed is sickening (literally), and one is forced to deal with imbeciles who assume that you are still "angry over the divorce." What I am angry about is being poor and being unemployed. It's not hard to be single. It's hard to be poor. Sixty years ago Virginia Woolf in *A Room of One's Own* reflected on "what effect poverty has on the mind. Why are women poor?" She referred to "the poison of fear and bitterness" and wisely declared, "What a change of temper a fixed income will bring about" (1929, 43).

SAVED BY FAITH

What has sustained me through ten years of poverty? My faith in an ever-loving, ever-present God, Jesus' words "not to worry" and His promise, "Whatever you need will be given to you."

I received a sense of mission from the high school study of Christ in the Gospel and the role modeling of teachers, some of whom I never met. In the 1960s I studied the spirituality of Charles de Foucauld (of the Little Brothers and Sisters of the Poor), but I did not expect to actually experience poverty. In the 1970s I collected at least two copies of each of the books of Ivan Illich. They opened my mind to question authority and the power of institutions. They suggested alternatives and more harmonious ways of being. I guess this was the preparation I needed for divorce and unemployment in the eighties. It was certainly not part of my plans. Faith has been the constant in my life, whatever my situation. Again and again I have been saved by faith!

I will tell you where I find fuel for the journey. Specifically, my long association with Holy Cross Centre, Port Burwell, Ontario, Canada has strengthened and enriched me. For me, this is home: Home is Holy. This is where I learned about respecting diversity, inclusivity, reciprocity, the celebration of life, wonder, mystery, passion, and the vision of a caring earth community. I'm still learning to walk gently on the earth. In recent years when I have felt truly stuck and battered by society and the institutions we have created I have found nurturance at several centers in the Province of Ontario: Avila Centre, Thunder Bay, and Loyola House, Guelph and Medaille Program Centre, London. For the wonderful people whose gift it is to enable others, I give thanks. At the top of the list would be Susan Maynard, my yoga teacher for five years, whose weekly classes, example, and friendship have never wavered, whatever my mental state, whether I had the money to pay or not. I also appreciate being a member of Mary Campbell Co-op housing. It's a great place to live! We are a mixed community. We value the diversity!

The people who help me are the ones who relate to me as an equal, who show compassion, respect, and humor. The majority of professionals have lost sight of what they are doing. They are busy filling out forms, looking for pathology, and trying to label, blame, and silence the victim. I'm reminded of the quotation from social justice, "We need the poor" so that the greedy can profit!

What drives me on is another quotation, "Our hope lies in the poor!" The poor, in liberating themselves, will liberate the oppressors as well. I celebrate when I see how many of us are discovering the new story.

II   Visions of Our Reality

The single life, like any other, has its own unique attributes, concerns, and challenges. It is the awareness of these that inspire the following women to respond realistically and wholeheartedly to the possibilities and limitations of their lives and to remain open to opportunities for change and growth.

Sheila Cassidy begins this section by sharing on an extremely personal basis her struggles to balance her spiritual self and her public contribution.

In "Affirming Myself: As Authentic Being, Friend, and Healer," Clare Christie presents the enriching aspects of the single life-style, not only to the individual herself but also to those with whom she comes into contact.

"Singleness," one of only two poems in the book, is a pithy vision by Betty Hares.

Divorced and in her thirties, Lin Collette chooses celibacy, in spite of the sacrifices, in order to maintain her integrity and to be her best person for both herself and others.

4   A Single Woman: The Fabric of My Life

Sheila Cassidy

When I was a little girl and, later on, an adolescent, it never occurred to me that I would not meet the man of my dreams, get married, and live happily ever after. Now, at fifty-four, it seems unlikely, though not impossible, that this will happen. It's not so much that hope springs eternal but that I have long since ceased predicting what shape or direction my life will take. The reality of my here and now, however, is that not only do I live alone but I actually *like* it. I value my space, my solitude, and my independence enormously and cannot readily envisage the circumstances that would lead me to want to change it. This is not to say that I do not enjoy company nor to deny that I am sometimes lonely—but most of the time I am deeply content with my way of life.

Before I go any further, let me explain what I mean by deeply content. I mean not so much constantly happy as peaceful at a deepest level of my being—at the level of who I really am. It has not always been thus. It has taken me many years to arrive at this place of interior peace, and although in the depths I remain still, my life is often storm tossed. Like the sea, its surface is sometimes choppy, sometimes mirror calm, and sometimes a roaring, terrifying chaos with waves as high as a mountain. Deep, deep down, however, things are still, because I know that I have somehow come home, have found a safe anchorage in the depths of the unseen God.

Even as I write them, these words seem both overpious and presumptuous, but I can think of no better way to put it. Let me tell you a little of my story, of how I came to this place, this way of being that I now call home.

I was the youngest of three children, conceived in my mother's late thirties at a time when, I suspect, she thought her nappy days were safely

over. One of the things that maddens me now, in my fifties, is the futility
of attempts at access to my childhood. The experience of psychotherapy
has taught me how pivotal are a person's early years—and yet my own
memories are locked away and my parents and their contemporaries long
since dead. There are tantalizing glimpses of a beautiful artistic woman
busy about many things, while a middle-aged nanny poured out love on
another woman's child. Then, in 1939, when I was two, war broke out.
My father, an officer in the Royal Air Force, was posted immediately to
London, and my mother, desperate to be with him, packed me off to my
grandparents and followed him.

Perhaps if the kindly nanny had accompanied me to Devon, things might
have been different: who knows? As it happened, however, I was placed
in the care of a raw sixteen-year-old servant girl and sent to the other end
of England, nearly three hundred miles away.

I have often wondered, these last few years, how it was for that little
girl of two, uprooted from all she recognized as secure and familiar,
landing in a household of rather stuffy adults. My grandparents were
people of the old school: genteel and formal, sticklers for right behavior
and a certain way of pronouncing the English language. The clearest
memory I have of my grandmother is a rebuke, a cutting parody of my
pronunciation in which the roundness of my vowels did not come up to
her expectations. I have, quite simply, no recall of the rest of that time.
There are photographs of me with my grandfather walking sedately around
the garden and a rather tearful portrait in my best dress but no spoor of the
nursemaid or the cook who were, I suspect, my closest companions in
those days when children were supposed to be seen but not heard.

I recount the tale of those early years because I now realize how
formative they must have been. Little children sent away from home are
incapable of understanding why. Their mothers may be dying, their worlds
may be in flames, they may be banished for their own protection: no matter.
All they know is that they have been sent away, that they are not wanted.
It's devastating, isn't it? You send your toddler off to your mother in the
country to save her from the bombs and in doing so you risk damaging her
infinitely more than if you cower with her night after night under the
kitchen table with the bombers droning overhead.

Let me elaborate. If you send your child away, she will *know* she is not
wanted. If she was good, she reasons, you would want her, but you clearly
don't, so she makes the only possible deduction that a two-year-old mind
can make: "I am unwanted and unloveable because I am of no worth."

It has long been known that not only is a small child's separation from
his or her mother extremely traumatic but, if the parent is not replaced by

a loving mother substitute, permanent psychological damage may ensue. A recent review of the literature by psychotherapist John Bowlby shows that children from loving stable homes are likely to grow up with a positive self-image, to be cheerful and socially cooperative citizens who are unlikely to break down in adversity. As adults, they are likely to form good stable marriages and to provide the same healthy environment for their children that they themselves enjoyed. Conversely, however, children whose early nurture has been deficient because of separation or inadequate parenting are likely to have a poor or negative self-image, to have difficulty with intimate relationships, and to be vulnerable in conditions of adversity.

I find these deductions chilling and ask myself, inevitably, Have I been damaged by those early years as a lonely child in that big house by the sea? The answer, if I am truthful, is probably yes. Perhaps I have indeed been scarred for life, had my potential for stable intimate relationships impaired, been made more vulnerable than some women to depressive illness. But that, of course, is not the whole story. If one side of my personality has been wounded by the accidents of my early rearing, there is no doubt that other dimensions have flowered. Had the later years of my childhood not been stable, things might have been very different, but I was lucky, and after those difficult three years away, I returned to my family and was cherished as a much-loved youngest child. I was lucky, too, to be good at my schoolwork, to be well educated and to be encouraged by both my parents and my teachers to stretch myself to the limits in a career of my own choosing. That I have been deeply fulfilled in my life and work as a doctor is, I know, riches indeed, but there is another dimension of my life, another branch that has borne much fruit in the last few years.

I refer here to the creative side of my life, to my joy and gift with words, both as a writer and as a preacher and lecturer. It is only in recent years that I have come to realize how pivotal is this creative activity to my happiness. My medical work is interesting, important, deeply fulfilling, but it is the artistic side of my endeavor that makes my heart sing, that makes me feel most vibrantly alive. When I muse, as I do from time to time, on the possibility of sharing my life with another person, the question that comes most urgently to mind is this: what would happen to my creative space, to that solitude, that freedom in which ideas and words are painstakingly crafted into that which has never before existed, into a piece of writing with a life of its own?

Where has it come from then, this demanding muse? I don't pretend it is very great: I simply acknowledge that it exists, that it shares my life and jealously protects its space, repelling all but the most transient of guests.

That many of my gifts are inherited, I have no doubt, for my mother was at core an artist, as were a long line of maiden aunts who drew, painted, and embroidered like angels. There is, however, another possibility: that the very deprivations of my childhood that stunted one side of my growth are in fact responsible for the flowering of this creativity. It is as though one of my legs was crippled by polio and the other has grown strong and muscular in order for me to walk.

It is only very recently that I have come to take seriously the possibility that my creative ability has developed not merely in spite of my woundedness but because of it in much the same way that a pruned tree will throw out new shoots.

It was the ideas contained in the Enneagram, an ancient method of defining personality types, that set me thinking along these lines. The origins of the Enneagram are mysterious, originating possibly with the Sufis, a mystical sect of Islam that began in the tenth and eleventh centuries. The ideas were transmitted in the oral tradition in the Middle East and were quite unknown in the West until this century. They have been explored and developed in Europe and the Americas until they have become a popular tool, especially in certain religious circles, for understanding human personality types.

My own information is gleaned from a book called *Personality Types* by ex-Jesuit Don Richard Riso. In his book, Riso describes the nine personality types of the Enneagram, outlining not only the characteristics of the "healthy" specimen of each different type but also the way in which each individual may move toward integration or disintegration of the personality.

I was particularly fascinated by his description of the childhood origins of the Type Four personality with which I personally identify. The Type Four is categorized as The Artist, and in its ideal state is "inspired and creative, expressing the universal in the human condition. Intuitive and thoughtfully self-aware. Self-revealing, personal, emotionally honest: serious and funny, sensitive and emotionally strong" (1987, 105). Riso sees such individuals emerging not from loving homes where their every little creative effort was applauded and encouraged but from a very different background. He sees them as the product of an unhappy or solitary childhood, lacking in role models and turning inward to their own feelings and imaginations:

From childhood, Fours felt essentially alone in life. It seemed to them that, for reasons they could not understand, their parents had rejected them, or at least that their parents did not take much interest in them. Fours felt, therefore, that there must be something deeply wrong with them, that they were somehow defective because their parents did not give them the kind of nurturing attentions which, as children, they needed. As a result, they turned to themselves to discover who they are (1987, 110).

Of all the personality types, says Riso, these wounded "Fours" are most in touch with the impulses from their unconscious minds. They have learned to listen to their inner voices while remaining open to impressions from the environment. He likens them to oysters, transforming all their experiences, painful and joyous alike, into something beautiful. More than anything, says Riso, their creativity is paradoxical because by opening themselves to their own depths, they access universal truths and make them available to everyone.

Let me confess before I am found out that I am only a dilettante and a dabbler in the world of the Enneagram, but what little I do know makes sense of my own experience, for I recognize myself at my creative best in the healthy Four and, alas, at my introspective, neurotic worst in the unhealthy version.

Myers-Briggs personality types were developed by Isobel Myers-Briggs and are based on the original descriptions of Carl Jung. I understand myself not only as a Myers-Briggs introverted intuitive INFP, but as an Enneagram Type Four, a person wounded from childhood, perhaps made a eunuch by circumstance, yet someone whose very wounds have flowered and borne much fruit.

Religious people sometimes talk about salvation history, the way events, joyous and painful, have molded a particular person's life, leading her in a certain direction and shaping her for her own unique destiny. I find reflection upon my own salvation history both fascinating and helpful, because not only does it make me very grateful but it confirms me in my belief that all things somehow, miraculously, work together for good.

After the first few rather traumatic years of my childhood, I was reunited with my family, and in 1949, when I was eleven, we emigrated to Australia. The years that followed were very happy, if rather isolated, for we lived on a small poultry farm on the outskirts of Sydney. It was during these adolescent years that my calling to medicine gradually became clear. Whether it came from reading too much A. J. Cronin or from a schoolgirl crush on the family doctor I am not sure, but I do know that at the age of fifteen I set out to be a doctor and I have never looked back.

In my last year at school, however, something happened that rocked me to my very foundations: I began to wonder if God was calling me to the religious life. I had been so sure not only that I was going to do medicine but also that I would marry and have children. Now it seemed that I was being asked to give up both these dreams, to let go the reins of my life and to submit to a way of living that I perceived as totally alien. I looked at the nuns in their black habits and veils and felt like a widow being led to the funeral pyre to commit suttee.

Despair made me bold, and I sought out a kindly priest and poured out my distress. How he must have smiled at the intensity and confusion of this solemn seventeen-year-old in her drab brown school uniform and panama hat, but I remember only that he took me seriously and helped me to understand that I must wait and discern what God was saying to me in the midst of such a violent interior storm.

As things turned out, I went on to university to study medicine, but the sense of being called, branded by God for service, never left me, and there were to be many reenactments of the conversation with the priest in the years to come.

By 1960 I was at Oxford University, my parents having returned to England, and after another heated skirmish with "vocationitis," I had settled down to complete my medical studies. It was here at Oxford, in my early twenties, that I met Michael Hollings, the Roman Catholic chaplain to the university who was to have a profound influence on my life. It was from Michael that I learned about prayer: not just how to do it or that fidelity and discipline are mandatory but that it was the wellspring of his power, the overwhelming joy of his life. Michael was, for me, an icon person, a man who was somehow especially alive and incandescent with the love of God. I have met other icon people over the years, men and women who have been like beacons along my way, constantly reaffirming me in my faith and tremulous certainty that God is all in all.

It took another Oxford friend, however, and a long period away from the church to widen my spiritual horizons and free me from the shackles of a particularly xenophobic and conservative upbringing. It was in 1965 that I met Consuelo Silva, a Chilean doctor who came to study in the department of plastic surgery where I was a resident. Consuelo was all the things that I was not: psychologically and politically aware, a socialist, an avid reader of English literature, and an atheist. Confined to the hospital during long hours of on call duty, we spent our time together, and she introduced me to Evelyn Waugh, to P. G. Wodehouse, to classical music, and to a world beyond my ken. How I had reached the age of thirty without taking in the existence of the Third World, I don't quite know, but Consuelo gently opened my eyes to the truths of poverty and injustice. Had I never met her, I am quite sure my life would have been very different; but we *did* meet and it was because of her that, when in search of an escape from the demands of the British medical rat race, I chose to go to Chile rather than Canada, New Zealand, or somewhere more conventional.

In November of 1971, therefore, I set out from Antwerp on a German cargo boat, taking with me my dog Winston and all my worldly goods. Five weeks later we disembarked at the port of Valparaiso and began an adventure that was to change both of our lives forever. The story of my Chilean experience has been told in *Audacity to Believe*; it is enough here to say that I stayed for four years, that I worked as a doctor among the very poor, that I was in Santiago during the 1973 military coup, and that in 1975 I was arrested and tortured for treating a wounded revolutionary. After three weeks in solitary confinement and five weeks in a concentration camp, I was released and sent back to England where, as the storybooks say, I have lived happily ever after.

Looking back towards those Chilean days, I can see that it is they, as much as my childhood, that have shaped the person I am today and the way that I live my life.

What does the experience of imprisonment and torture do to a human being? Perhaps inevitably, it separates me a little from other people because it makes them uncomfortable when they think about what I have suffered. Christopher Holdsworth, Public Orator at Exeter University, wrote about me recently (1991) that I might be, for some people, a disturbing person since I had experienced things that most of us would hope to escape and since in my normal profession I work in the presence of that ultimate experience, death. "Such a life, on the margins of the bearable, poses questions which we know not how to address."

Do I live my life on the margins of the bearable? I don't know. What I do know is that I have put my hand into the wounded side of the world, and perhaps there is still blood on it. Perhaps I am too familiar with the reality of hunger, oppression, torture, and death to be easy company. Most people would like me to speak at their prize-giving ceremony but not come home to dinner. As it happens, this suits me well enough. Perhaps my prison experience has left me with an uncomfortable directness of speech and little patience with small talk. It's true that I'm useless at cocktail parties; but it's also true that with people whose values I share, with whom I feel comfortable, I am enormously happy. It's not that we necessarily talk about "heavy" issues but that there is a shared understanding that makes frivolity, satire, or deep things of the spirit equally acceptable.

My friendships, then, tend to be with men and women who are involved in one way or another with those who suffer. They are people who, like me, have experienced the darkness of depression or exhaustion and for whom success and failure are often intertwined. More than anything, they are people who speak the same kind of faith language. It's not that I seek out religious people or that we necessarily talk much about faith issues but that there is a deep sense of homecoming in being with people for whom the love of God is central rather than peripheral.

The experience of community is a crucial part of my life as a single person. I was raised with the ordinary understanding of the word "community": a group of people living under the same roof, sharing their goods and their lives for better or for worse. Religious life in community was always held up to me as a wonderful way of living the Gospel, and it's only in fairly recent years that I have heard people speak of the very real difficulties experienced by those who live under the same roof. I remember a monk friend saying that living in community is like being in a pebble grinder—after years and years of rubbing painfully up against each other, people become smoother, but the process is exquisitely painful. Jean Vanier (1989) says that the essence of community is not that the people in it are either attracted or suited to each other but that they are called and bonded together because of a desire to work for a common cause. Without that common cause, a community becomes inward looking and eventually disintegrates.

My own experience of community has been fourfold: two months in a prison camp with one hundred other political prisoners, eighteen months in a convent with about twenty other women, ten years in the hospice where I now work, and many years of loose friendship with men and women the world over whose values I share. What then have I learned?

There is no doubt that my experience of prison community was a rich one. I was with a brave group of strong women, nearly all of whom had been imprisoned and tortured because they were working to improve the conditions of the poor. The discipline in the community was strong, and there was a selflessness I have not met elsewhere. I came to love those women deeply, and I count myself truly privileged to have lived amongst them.

The convent was different, very different, and I was not very happy. I was both bitterly lonely for kindred spirits and constrained by the demands of a polite all-female society. It seemed that everything I did was wrong, and I found myself unable to conform without intolerable strain. After eighteen months I was asked to leave because I was so unhappy; I know now that it was the right decision. At the time, however, I thought I could make it work because I did not realize that I am personally unsuited to community life.

So the convent threw me out and I returned to the world to lick my wounds. Not to be outwitted in my attempts to be Holier than Everyone,

I set myself up as a hermit in a trailer on my brother's farm. Each morning I rose early to say my prayers; then, borrowing my brother's car (it being against my ideas of poverty to buy my own), I drove to the nearby town for Mass. After Mass, I was hungry, so I bought coffee and went for a little stroll around the shops. Soon I was hungry again, so I bought lunch and sat by the river to eat my sandwiches and think spiritual thoughts. This routine worked well for about six weeks, and then I ran out of money. At first I determined to do a few general practice surgeries to earn my keep. I soon realized I was unfitted even for this and that the only thing I could do was to be a junior resident in the hospital. It wasn't difficult to get a locum post, and on July 1, 1980, I returned to British medicine after a gap of nine years.

To my great surprise and inner laughter, I found myself completely at home. No one seemed to mind the way I walked or dressed and no one complained about my language. To my amazement, I found the staff valued the way I worked with patients. Within a week I had been offered a permanent post. Slowly, I realized that I had come home. The hospital corridor was my cloister, and my heart sang with thanksgiving as I clattered noisily down it. Here, at last, in my white coat and bright shirts I merged into the crowd, and no one minded that my desk was cluttered or that I was always breathlessly a few minutes late instead of serenely early.

After eighteen months of working on the cancer wards in the general hospital, I was offered a job as medical director of a new hospice for the terminally ill, and early in 1982, I took up the post. Now, after ten years, I realize that I have, quite inadvertently, acquired my own community. Although by no means the Mother Superior, I have a considerable leadership role and suffer the joys and hardships inseparable from belonging to a group of people. I believe that this hospice community fulfils Jean Vanier's criteria: we are a group of disparate and often incompatible people called to live our lives together because we are united by a common cause. In this lies both our strength and our weakness. We are strong because we work single-mindedly as a team, weak when we fight and hurt each other. I have over my desk a quotation from Martin Luther King that reads, "Unless we work together as brothers, we shall perish together as fools." Sometimes I believe we have come near to perishing, but the strength of our commitment to the work has saved us, and we have reengaged at a deeper level, evermore conscious of our woundedness and fragility.

On a practical level, I believe the strength of our community lies precisely in the fact that we do not live together. When the work is done we go home to wives, families, lovers or, a few of us, to our solitary apartments or houses. It is only in recent years that I have come to understand the enormous importance of my home. It is not just the physical base where I sleep and keep my belongings—it is an extension of myself, the place of my creativity, of my security, of my hidden life. It is the place where I can be most totally myself: a chaotic, creative, untidy, and deeply religious woman. If I want people to understand my work as a doctor, I invite them to the hospice—but if I want them to know who I really am, I bring them to my home.

I delighted in Christopher Holdsworth's (1991) recent description of my three-roomed flat high above Plymouth's sea front:

The splendid chaos of her main living room, rather like a windy ship's saloon, demonstrates as she said to me, that she is one of a long line of people who don't like keeping things tidy (she actually used rather more robust language) but she also cherishes the beautiful: a large copper jug found in Fiesole, a glass roundel of Noah and his Ark copied from the original at Chartres, a Rublev's Icon of the Trinity. . . . Beauty, chaos and a curious sense of space and peace have been created in that ship-like room. Perhaps, together they symbolize important aspects of her whole life.

My interviewer was a shrewd man, for the chaos, the beauty, and the icon are indeed symbols of who I am and what is important to me. The chaos is a product of a life packed full with different endeavors: writing, sewing, reading, cooking, praying, and a delight in the freedom to abandon washing up and cleaning in favor of some more entertaining pursuit. (You can see I would make a very tiresome roommate!) The artistic objects in my house are part of a newfound freedom and understanding of my need for color and for the beautiful. How I ever thought I could survive in the aesthetic desert of a convent I do not know. Lastly, the icon with its candle is the sign that this is the room not only where I cook and eat, entertain, and watch television but also where I pray.

Work, prayer, creativity, friendship, rest: these are the threads from which the fabric of my life is being woven. I can only hope that the knots, the holes, and the twisted yarns will add to the eventual glory of the cloth! Meanwhile, I am acutely conscious of the difficulty of getting the pattern right.

This difficulty of balancing the various parts of my life has, for a number of years, been my greatest problem. Each year I naively think I'll get it right—but each year I am forced to acknowledge that my life is in some respects a mess. When I wrote earlier of the intertwining of triumph and failure, I was speaking from my own experience. During the course of the past year I have published a new book, been awarded an honorary degree, conducted a day of prayer in Westminster Abbey, preached in about five different cathedrals, received a literary award, and had the most difficult year ever of conflict with the people with whom I work. I have been rebuked like a naughty child for my language and have been so afraid of losing my job, I could have been sick in the street. I have been so depressed that I sat before an open window considering throwing myself out of it and had to seek help in order to regain my equilibrium. Perhaps it's just as well that I am single, or I would have to add a broken marriage to this tale of woes!

Now, as I lick my wounds and try to work out where things went wrong, I find it absurdly difficult to arrive at a satisfactory solution. Part of the trouble is that I long for an all or nothing answer: stop doing this, cancel that. This is a sin; that is God's will. But life is never that simple. I know that I have been away from the hospice more than was good for it or for me. That at least is clear. But that does not negate the good of what I did whilst away. Am I to say that lecturing about the care of the dying in Singapore, East Germany, Spain, Hong Kong was useless? Of course not. Nor will I deny that it was fun—loads of fun most of the time. But it was costly, very costly, because of stress, jet lag, exhaustion, all those undeniable pressures that go with high-profile work and foreign travel. So, as I go back to the drawing board, I cannot say, "I will be good and stay at home!" That would be death to my creative spirit and a denial of my teaching gifts; but I know I must count the cost of what I do much more carefully in the future.

I know that I am not alone in experiencing this difficulty in discerning the balance between mission at home and away, but I suspect that each person must find his or her own answer and that the answer may differ from time to time. One of the factors that I had not previously taken into account is the need that the base community has for its key members. I thought that because my unit was adequately staffed, it was safe for me to be away, but I learned to my cost that this was not so. I was missed not because the work was not being done but because of something much less easy to define or name: a quality of leadership or presence that made people feel secure.

So this year I have, with much pain, learned a new lesson, that I who think of myself as a free spirit, belonging to no one, do in fact "belong" to a considerable extent to the community of people with whom I work. It has taken me some time to adjust to this knowledge and to move from resenting the bonds that hold me to both valuing and enjoying that belonging. Perhaps I am learning at last that we all need a degree of rootedness if we are to flower and bear fruit worth sharing.

The other conflict that I am trying to resolve is between the demands of my medical work and my writing. Once again, it would be so much easier if things were cut and dried, if I could discern that I should give up medicine and become a full-time writer. Mercifully, however, I have enough insight to realize that my writing is a secondary gift and that I actually need to work with people for it to flower. There is also the very pragmatic issue that I could not earn enough to live on if I gave up medicine—let alone run my car and travel abroad as is my wont! My solution, when I find it, will no doubt be yet another compromise involving the rearranging of commitments rather than any radical change. Pity! I have a secret penchant for dramatic gestures like going off on a cargo boat to South America or abandoning the world to enter a convent!

The other area of my life that has been a source of conflict in the past is what is loosely called life-style. I am speaking here not so much of the balance of work and leisure but of standard of living, how one allocates one's resources. This issue, which has taxed me for many years, is at the moment on the back burner of my priorities. Most of the time it simmers quietly away, and from time to time I take the lid off and have a look at it. My notion of how I should live my life took a massive knock in Chile when I saw for myself not only how the poor live but how the American and Irish missionaries lived. I'll never forget the day I went to lunch with two American priests and, being sent to a bedroom to fetch a chair, had a glimpse of their life-style. There was a spare shirt and a pair of jeans on a nail behind the door—and that was all. I couldn't believe it, and I was tormented by it for years as I replayed to myself the story of Christ's call to the rich young man: "If you would be perfect, go sell what you have, give it to the poor, and come follow me" (Matt. 19:21). That story has been the undoing of a lot of good people: Antony, the father of Egyptian monasticism, Augustine, and Lord knows who else. And I, did I too not want to be perfect? What was wrong with me that I couldn't sell all and follow?

The story of my struggles with mammon is a long and sometimes a funny one. I had a serious attempt at the simple life when I left the convent. "Who needs a washing machine?" I said, and my clothes got greyer and greyer; "Who needs a television?" I protested—until "Brideshead Revisited" was aired and I capitulated. "*Never*," I said, "will I own a work of art worth more than a hundred pounds"—until I bought a Persian rug for six hundred pounds. Once, sickened by my own materialism, I went on a clothes fast for a year; no new clothes, not even new tights. It lasted nine months, quite something for a pathological shopper like me, but then one day on a wild Scottish Island, I came across a lone Hebridean girl at her knitting machine. As I looked across at the mountains, it seemed a sin not to support her, so I broke my fast and bought the sweater she had just finished.

Sweaters are my undoing; I love them! One day I came across this scrap of my prose from a never-finished essay: "Last week I bought five sweaters: one red, one blue, one green and one grey. Last week we had five deaths: one 42, one 36, two 55 and one 17. I wonder is there any connection?"

Then at last I saw it. My present work is indeed on the margins of the bearable, for walking day by day toward the gates of death makes enormous demands upon my personal reserves and vitality. I remember with exceptional clarity one weekend when I was particularly low. As I sat in tears trying to pull myself together, the phone rang; it was a doctor asking me if I would visit a young man who was dying and was afraid to meet God. I groaned but said yes, and set off to drive the fifteen or so miles to where the man lived. After I had talked to him, I decided to treat myself to a stroll around the shops. I met my downfall, for in a narrow alleyway I came across a very special sweater shop. Two hours later not only had I made a new friend and acquired two hand-knitted "designer" woollies but I was cured of my depression: my heart sang and I felt full of energy.

I've thought a lot about those sweaters as I've struggled with the voices from the back burner. At first I was convinced it was a sin to spend so much money on one sweater (let alone two!) Then my thoughts went like this: if it's a sin for *me* to buy this sweater, is it a sin for *anybody* to buy it? What about the girl who knitted it? And what about Kaffe Fassett, the artist who designed the garment? Who am I to say he should bury his God-given talents just because I feel guilty paying for the labor of someone who makes a work of art? So after a while, I came to the conclusion that I am not too holy to buy a beautiful hand-knit and that I should quite simply rejoice and be glad in it.

Returning to my theme of weaving the fabric of life and reflecting upon the most important strands, the woof (or is it the warp?) of my existence is my relationship with God. I've thought a lot over the years about the issues of singleness in general and celibacy in particular in relation to my life with God. For a long time I thought I was being called to a life of celibacy because I was wanted by God in a special relationship. I saw this, as many people do, as analogous to a marriage, and my call seemed to be either to union with God or to union with a man. Once, in the course of a retreat, I made a vow of chastity for one year. The night before I made the vow I had a dream: I had slashed a great piece out of my breast and cobbled the wound together with a thick nylon tension suture. I was very unnerved, but went ahead.

As things happened, I didn't keep my promise. Now, the way things are, I could make the vow again, but I don't feel any particular need to. I suppose I no longer see union with God as being a sexual issue: if I did, how could I explain the closeness to God of my many married friends, clergy and lay?

My understanding of God has much more to do with a love that transcends the sexual, although it can be likened to it. I see union with God as a union of wills, a cleaving of the soul to God that requires discipline and fidelity to prayer and an ongoing discernment of how to live one's life in relation to others. What my singleness does is make it possible for me to earmark a degree of time and space for God that might not be possible if I were married. It's not that I spend long tracts of time each day in prayer but that there is a certain space in my life that allows me room for things of the spirit. The half hour I spend each morning, the ten minutes at night, before my Rublev icon would be just that much more difficult if I was searching for my children's missing shoes or socks as well as my own.

And lastly, the inevitable question: does my relationship with God totally fill the void of my aloneness? The answer is both yes and no. There are days when my heart and my loins ache for another human being to share my life, but these moments have been much fewer in recent years. Instead, there is a deep and quiet joy that is difficult to describe, but can be summed up in the words of the psalmist:

> Your love is better than life,
> my lips will speak your praise. (Psalm 62)

5 Affirming Myself: As Authentic Being, Friend, and Healer

Clare Christie

Last week my twenty-seven-year-old roommate told me that the example of my fulfilling single life had given her the courage to break up with her boyfriend of four years about whom she still felt serious reservations. Yesterday I was seized with major pangs of wishing for a congenial male partner with whom to share a gemlike autumn afternoon. But here I am, today, ready to affirm the single state and to call for its celebration in our culture as a sign of authenticity, resourcefulness, and strength, desirable qualities in women and men alike.

As an ever-single woman I am part of the group that is valued the least among (white) women in our society.

The fact that I don't buy into this devalued image is a tribute to my upbringing, my family and friends, and myself. But those same family and friends, that same self, have never affirmed and celebrated my singleness.

For too long the practice has been to explain the state of singleness by finding fault with the single person. It is time to debunk this idea, as many single people are no more dificult to live with than many married people. As a sociable, ever-single person in my midforties, I have had the opportunity to live with a series of roommates and to befriend many single persons. Trying to identify why any one of them is single or why I am, is rarely a constructive process, whereas singing the praises of these individuals and their contributions (and my own) is easy and uplifting.

I have always believed in making the best of the situation in which I find myself, and I have found that there are usually benefits, if not joys, to be found. There are many benefits, joys, and advantages to being single, and I am not referring to being selfish and lazy.

As an ever-single, I have had the opportunity to truly become my own person. I have had to take the responsibility for my decisions and actions and have been forced into honesty. As I have made my choices in life, there was no one else to either blame or to credit.

In solitude I have come to know myself psychologically, intellectually, and spiritually. Physically as well. I have the discretion to take the time to go through the process. I have the opportunity to listen to feedback from family and friends that pertains to me, rather than to endless discussions about my relationship with my man or my children. Solitude has given me the opportunity to pass through pain to growth.

To be a complete person is not dependent upon a lasting marriage relationship (notice that I didn't write "happy") but upon a well-developed sense of self-esteem, a personal strength of integrity—without smugness or intolerance. Wholeness, or authenticity, is integration of mind, body and spirit.

AUTHENTICITY

My upbringing and disposition have meant that I have had enough self-confidence, even during the hard times, to proceed with honesty and effort so that either I haven't been hit hard enough yet to keep me down (and there have been some wallops) or else my attitude that it could have been worse gives me an optimistic perspective. There is no question that my self-confidence stems from the love and security that I not only experienced in a happy childhood but also have continued to experience with my family and friends.

I was fortunate to grow up in a family where I was both loved and given enough independence to learn early a sense of myself and to feel good about it. I was taught to accept my differences from other little girls—that I was tall, learned to read without effort, was a tomboy, and preferred active, outdoor pursuits to playing indoors with dolls—and my mother even let me wear nothing but swimming trunks all summer until I was embarrassed by the first signs of my developing breasts. I asked to play the drums in rhythm band in Grade 4 and was the first girl to do so, as I recall. My best friends in this prepubertal period were boys, and two of them are still among my most special people.

Although I was very sensitive to peer pressure during puberty and in my early teens, I think my childhood gave me the strength to say no to smoking after trying it a few times at age eleven and not enjoying it. I cut out kissing, too, from just before my twelfth birthday until just before my sixteenth, and the boy who kissed me good-bye at the end of that summer, still a special friend, did me a real favor with that friendly, affectionate surprise kiss. The point is that I had the courage to live by my own principles, those that seemed right for me, rather than by the expectations of my peer group.

I was aware during the sixties, while at university, that in the male-female relationships I saw forming around me, there was an overriding sense that the partner was to be considered one's fulfillment, which meant no friendships with the opposite sex. I remember feeling very strongly that I would rather be single than accept such a condition, probably because my male childhood friends were so dear to me. My relationships with men have always been based on an acceptance of other friends and, consequently, on trust.

Joseph Campbell, the American mythologist, always told his students to follow their bliss (1988, 118–121). This is the best path to authenticity, but it can only be done if one shields oneself from the demands of societal pressures. At the end of my undergraduate years, I had a flurry of friends with engagement rings, but I felt no envy. I had been bitten by the travel bug and had always intended to travel as soon as I was free of my parents' expectation, which was to graduate. I remember thinking that as I didn't want to be an old maid, which I figured happened at twenty-five, I would marry on Labor Day weekend, 1971, days before my twenty-fifth birthday, but in the meantime I planned to pack in as much travel and adventure as I could. I managed the adventures, but I picked up mononucleosis as a result, not a husband!

One of the reasons I celebrate my singleness is that I cherish the opportunity to be my authentic self. I affirm that I desire always to be "single" in the sense of my uniqueness, even as I long to share with other "singles," of both sexes, all sexual orientations, religions, races, ages, and physical and mental capacities, and whatever their marital status.

In sharing on an authentic, intimate level, I meet my God, the goodness in all people, and I feel blessed.

RISK TAKING

In the course of the adventures I have referred to, I have been free to take more risks because there is only my own safety or well-being to consider. Because these decisions have almost always led to positive experiences, my adventures have been wonderful, and I have emerged with an optimistic view of people. I am cautious enough not to be foolhardy, but I have traveled alone, meeting new individuals and groups of people, and I enjoy trying new experiences and considering new ideas. This, to my mind, is one of the great advantages of singlehood that should be celebrated, even trumpeted!

A recent risk was my decision to share with a wide range of people significant in my life my spiritual journey, which is ecumenical in the traditional sense and encompasses New Age interests. To my knowledge, many of the 150 people who received my letter were not concerned about the spiritual dimension of their experience, while others appeared to be comfortable only within their clearly defined religious frameworks. For reasons that I do not take personally, many recipients have not responded. Among the many who have, there has been a wide range of response, but with only one exception, those who have responded have been appreciative of the sharing and honesty involved. In numerous cases they have rewarded me with a return of intimacy by offering their perspective, in verbal or written form, and by gifts of books that have been important to them.

It is my observation that female or male, young or old, single or married, all respond on some level to authenticity in others. So my friends who may not have thought about the spiritual or ethical issues I raised, may not have been comfortable with them, or may have disagreed with me, still responded to the fact that I cared enough about them to share my deepest feelings with them.

As I write, a three-story mural is being painted on the outside wall of my historic house, which is on one of Halifax's main thoroughfares. The artist is presenting in pictorial form a list of changes I would like to see in society, ranging from a celebration of the feminine in public life to democracy in China. The depiction of a homosexual marriage is one of the more controversial subjects. The concept captured my enthusiasm (and my pocketbook) in a way a typical historical scene had failed to do, so I find myself making a public statement of my values for anyone who cares to interpret it. The mural is not designed to win me friends or clients—but the risk of losing them is mine to run. However, approval will also be mine to enjoy (with due credit to Jenni Blackmore, the artist).

I have no doubt that these adventures of relationship, mind, and spirit have deepened my sense of myself, of my spirituality, and of God/Christ in me.

HEALING AND FECUNDITY

Although the burdens of life may seem more onerous if borne singly, it is really a matter of attitude. If I see my single state as a subject of celebration, I enjoy the advantages of it; if I see my single state as a sign of my failures and faults, I will wallow in self-pity and shun the company of others. The latter approach will, of course, add to my burdens, while the former approach will attract friends only too glad to share and to lighten my occasional difficulties.

When I'm in a caretaking or service capacity, I need care myself, and in any case I need time to maintain my support network. I need to know to whom I can turn, no matter how independent I appear. My self-sufficiency has limits, much as I have to contribute. I need fun, humor, and joy in my life. I feel intensely.

As a single person, I have great potential to be a healer, in the sense of being a true friend. Not only is the path to my own authenticity easier because I don't have a partner to constantly consider but I can also make myself more readily available for listening, holding, caring, supporting. And I can reorder my priorities and time commitments instantaneously, often without the necessity of consulting anyone else.

Authenticity is the sign of someone who has come to terms with herself, her dark side as well as the light, who has had the opportunity to live with herself in an accepting, loving relationship, and who is willing to risk sharing herself with others. Such a person is a natural healer because she encourages the other also to accept and to love herself and to take the same risk. This is the compliment paid me by the roommate that I referred to in my opening paragraph, articulate and aware as she is about the forces that are competing in her.

Fecundity is not only a matter of bearing and raising children. Loving others to growth and receiving their love, allowing them the gift of giving, is a fecundity denied to no one. In my singleness, I affirm my capacity to love and to be loved. Next time I'm asked, "How's your love life?" I'll respond that it is abundant and rich in its variety!

FRIENDSHIPS

As a single person, I do not need to get into discussion about the desirability of developing a friendship with a particular person. I am friendly with old, young, homosexuals, those of other races, persons with AIDS and with mental handicaps and am able to spend time with any of my friends as determined by our mutual feelings for each other, not by the demands of my spouse or children, who might not share my interest in their company.

It is simpler for others to relate to me intimately because of my single status. I have no partner whose needs they should consider; there is no one else they have to trust. I am more readily available to meet, to call, or to correspond with than a family person, so a dialogue is more readily entered into, which deepens our relationship.

One of the great advantages of being single is surely this availability. Summer in Atlantic Canada is always a flurry of Come from Awayers or, the expression I prefer, Visiting Friends and Relatives (VFRs). I have no one else's schedule to mesh with in finding time to visit and so have been able to maintain over the years a lengthy list of VFRs with whom I feel a real closeness. I also have been able to plan occasional holidays specific-ally to visit old friends who can usually accommodate a single person in their homes and whose focus I then don't have to share with my spouse or children. The smaller the number, the deeper the sharing tends to be, in my experience—wonderful as group memories can be.

Other ever-single women relate to me more candidly than they would to someone who had been married, and women who are presently single feel that we share a great deal, but it is probably in my relationships with married men that my single status makes the biggest difference. It is a real advantage that there are no male partner's concerns to be taken into account, although there can be the fear, on the part of either of us, of creating an impression of illicit intimacy. Perhaps it is a function of age that this does not seem to get in the way very much anymore, but I have also long believed that the truth of the situation is what is important. It seems to me that it is a compliment to another woman for me to admire her husband as long as it is equally clear that I have no designs on him. As the years pass and my friends' marriages deepen, my opportunities to share very personal conversations with my old male friends increase. I treasure these occasions.

It is remarkable to me how the quality of a friendship is affected by the medium of communication. One of my closest friends had been a buddy for years, part of a group who did many fun things together. One evening on a camping trip, we sat in the dark beside the lake and had our first one-on-one conversation in which she talked about her difficult childhood. Immediately my feelings for her deepened. Shortly after that I was away from Halifax for three years and we corresponded, adding another valuable dimension to our relationship.

I suspect few people today carry on correspondence, but there is no doubt in my mind that it is a valuable tool for sharing with another person in a way that is not likely to happen in conversation. I mailed and gave the letter about my spiritual journey to people in Halifax with whom I live, work, and play and to whom I have never written before. Many of them said they wanted to respond in writing in order to thoughtfully express ideas they weren't accustomed to discussing or even to articulating.

Because I maintain a large correspondence, for several years I have resorted to copied letters sent out once a year or so, usually with a personal, handwritten section added. I hesitated to resort to copied letters, but friends' examples showed me that if the contents are honest and meaningful, a copied letter is greatly preferable to minimal communication.

As someone with an insatiable interest in how others think and live, these windows into the lives of others on a meaningful level, even briefly, are for me truly a blessing of the single state.

MARRIAGE

Marriage, meaning a relationship between loving companions—spiritual, emotional, physical, intellectual, and social accompanying.

I always expected to marry, I still hope to marry, but the thought that I might have been one of those so lacking in self-confidence and so dissatisfied with my own company that I would have married just to be married appalls me, and I say that believing that I, too, could be married if marriage was that important to me.

I really do believe that many young people marry to reassure themselves about themselves. I now practice law, handling especially divorce clients, so I have an excellent opportunity to benefit from their hindsight. Some couples simply grow apart, but many tell me that they were complying with expectations they felt from family and society and, consequently, themselves. I think I, and many others who didn't marry in our early twenties, deserve credit for not being as susceptible to these pressures.

Single people would be well advised to live life to the fullest with what they have at hand—themselves—rather than operating with a "camping mentality", ready to pull up stakes when a potential mate materializes. Years can pass while many other kinds of opportunities are missed.

I also have experienced my share of heartbreak, but respect the two men in question, not to mention partners from whom I suffered lesser hurts, for the qualities they showed in breaking off relationships that were not allowing them to be true to themselves (one of the hazards of falling in love with self-knowing people!).

Sexual intimacy, especially in marriage, would be the ultimate sharing, but to find a "single," a whole person who is also male, unmarried, heterosexual, and local, feels at times a little like believing that fairy tales do come true. Sometimes they do, but in the meantime, as an uncoupled single, I can make my own decisions about developing and balancing my glorious opportunities: for solitude, for a wealth of intimacy with my family and friends, and for my professional life.

CONCLUSION

It is time for society and all individuals who comprise society, including we singles ourselves, to affirm and even to celebrate the single state and to articulate an ideal for the single person as our culture does for the family. My suggestion is an ideal of the single person as an authentic human being, an available and true friend, a healer in the community.

Couples who don't develop single friends miss a great resource! (Whether we're heterosexual or homosexual, what difference should it make if we're not about to copulate?)

The worth of the single individual should be recognized, and single people should be made to feel accepted. Public and social functions should be planned so that all individuals feel welcomed. It should be acceptable for people to go to public events by themselves, to attend social functions without an escort, to remain single, to divorce, and to be widowed.

The Christian message encourages authenticity by teaching that God loves us as we are and by urging us to value relationships rather than material acquisitions and prestige. Maybe my singleness is part of God's plan for me, and I should consciously try to make a contribution as a person who is single. That would mean that writing this article, co-editing this book, acting as a positive role model are all part of God's call: truly a thought worth celebrating.

6 Singleness

Betty Hares

Singleness
is the liberty
to be me,
to do what I like
when I like,
to travel
unencumbered
the highways
of the world.

Singleness
is the discipline
of freedom,
the privilege
of having more time
for others,
more responsibility
to give myself,
more space
to share.

Singleness
is the pain
of children
never born,
of being
on the outside

of family,
mysteriously virgin,
threatening to others.

Singleness
is aloneness
in my one-person family,
the open door
and table,
the discovery
that I am loved,
valued and of value.

Singleness
is the ache
of rejection,
bereavement,
desertion,
of having
no living body
to throw my arms around
and love me
for myself alone.

Singleness
is the ability
to close my front door
on the world,
to enjoy my solitude,
listen to music,
paint,
be at peace.

Singleness
is my beginning
and my end,
my laughter
and my tears,
myself and God,
complete,
loved and loving,
at home and free,
celebrate with me!

7 Creating a Separate Space: Celibacy and Singlehood

Lin Collette

Since childhood, I have loved to play solitaire, a card game that has relaxed me and has provided much thinking time. I suppose that my love for this and other games or sports that are usually played by one person foreshadowed my adult love for solitude and my habit of being a loner. I think also that it has been a predictor of my decision to live the rest of my life alone, without a permanent intimate relationship with another person, and to live the rest of my life as a celibate person.

But making, and then living, this decision has not been without pain. In the five years since, I have given up a relationship that I found fulfilling because my partner was uncomfortable with my decision and could not continue seeing me without there being some physical intimacy. This has caused me great pain over the years, and my loneliness has sometimes been intense, as I face the reality of having no one to come home to—ever. Yet at the same time, I have felt as if I have been given a gift, as if I can transform active sexuality into an energy that can be given to others through service.

My decision to be celibate is not something I've felt comfortable discussing with people, since sexuality is such a loaded issue for single people, especially women. I am a divorced woman in my thirties and so it is assumed by others and by pollsters that I am sexually active. If I'm not, then I certainly must want to be sexually active with a special person so that I can be considered "normal" by my peers.

The necessity of having a sexual relationship with someone—anyone— in order to feel whole, is such a pervasive theme in society that it's understandable why single people who choose to be chaste or even celibate feel like fish out of water, especially when spinsters and celibates are portrayed by the various media as tortured souls denying an essential part of their reality or as meddlesome idiots who have nothing to do with their time but bother others.

I think of books written by my favorite authors, Dorothy Sayers, Ngaio Marsh, and P. D. James, in which spinsters are usually one-dimensional individuals with few variances in character. They are often repressed or silly (such as Miss Climpson in Sayers's Peter Wimsey series or Miss Emily Wharton in P. D. James's *A Taste for Death*). Or they can be gullible (such as the naive women who fall prey to religious cults in *Death in Ecstasy* or *Spinsters in Jeopardy*, both by Ngaio Marsh). Or, often, they are vindictive individuals (i.e., the Misses Prentice and Campanula of Ngaio Marsh's *Overture to Death*). Rarely are spinsters portrayed as human beings who lead full and satisfying lives. Rather, they are women to be pitied because they are alone and presumably unhappy.

Even women alone through divorce or widowhood are seldom shown to have interesting lives. Although the sitcom "The Golden Girls" is supposed to be about how four elderly single women find each other and live together as a "family," in a number of instances it has portrayed its characters as alternately silly, sex-starved, mean or absentminded. It's no wonder that our beliefs that single women of any age or circumstance are abnormal or flawed have changed little, with examples such as these being used as the norm.

In her book *Purity Makes the Heart Grow Stronger: Sexuality and the Single Christian*, Julia Duin talks about her struggle to remain chaste in a society many people see as permissive. She says:

Many of our friends consider life without sex abnormal. If we are divorced or widowed, they wonder why we don't use our newfound freedom to explore sexual frontiers. If we used to sleep around before conversion but now do not, people wonder why we are acting virtuous all of a sudden. (15)

Society, in her opinion, "expects that everyone needs and wants sex. The unmarried are portrayed as sexually active on most TV sitcoms. Sex between the unmarried is considered normal, accepted, and fashionable" (16).

My own discussions with friends, family, and workmates bear this out. If you're single, you must be on the prowl and having a wonderful time. I can't count the number of times people I know have asked me in conversation if I'm being "satisfied" by whomever I'm seeing, and they are nonplussed and confused when I tell them that I'm not seeing anyone and am happy that way. My relatives always ask *when* (not if) I'm getting married again and don't understand why dating doesn't seem to interest me. They assume that something must be wrong and that I must be going crazy because I'm not dating.

The truth is somewhat different from what they imagine. As a relatively young woman, I've chosen to live celibate, to permanently abstain from sexual relationships, for the rest of my life. I have not made this choice in order to enter a religious order in which such a life-style would be de rigueur, although I would be overjoyed if I someday felt called to enter a religious order. Nor has the fear of AIDS prompted me to decide against engaging in sexual relationships—even monogamous ones. And it's not for lack of opportunity.

My decision comes out of a dissatisfaction with sexual relationships and how they affect my interior life. When involved with someone, I found it difficult to justify taking time to work on my own projects and to have a truly private life, free from prying eyes. My partners always wanted to be involved in all facets of my life and resented my need for privacy. I was accused of being selfish. I admit here that selfish is what I need to be at this stage of my life. By choosing celibacy, by choosing not to become part of a union of two people, I am choosing autonomy—because I have found it difficult to maintain my otherness as part of a couple and have ended up sacrificing my own self in favor of my partner. While that might have been satisfactory at another stage of my life, it is not permissible now.

One of the most serious running arguments during my marriage was, in fact, my need to write and read and to maintain my own identity. My ex-husband felt that these activities kept him at a distance, although I tried to involve him whenever I could. There were times, however, when I could not—when I needed to absent myself in order to do a particularly troublesome piece of work—and his resentment grew every time I did this. In relationships entered into after my divorce, at a time when I was working and going to school full-time, I found that the time spent in nurturing relationships took time and energy away from my studies—studies that were important for me to be able to move ahead with my life. Again, my partners were resentful of the time spent away from them, and it was difficult to find a solution that pleased both of us.

I should say here, too, that I have nothing against sexual relationships or sexuality—for other people. I think marriage or some other form of committed relationship is a grand idea—for other people. Choosing to be celibate doesn't dictate an end to a sexual life, however, as I've found that my sexuality is very much present. I am sometimes sexually stimulated by different things, but I am learning to channel those feelings into a greater appreciation of what I see around me, into a sensuous regard for the world, one might say.

Indeed, according to the spiritual writer Benedict Groeschel, celibacy is a form of sexuality, as he says in his book *The Courage to be Chaste*: "Mere sexual abstinence is an expression of repression of unrealism and realism. Every mature person has to be realistic about sexuality, no one more so than someone trying to lead a chaste single life" (42).

Since choosing not to be involved with sexual relationships, I have found much needed time and energy to do that work which is vital to me. The passion that I once poured into my relationships, I now put into my work. Indeed, I feel relief that I can devote my heart and soul to that which I need to do, and I find I am not alone. May Sarton, in her book *At Seventy*, says that she is grateful to have reached that stage: "I have felt immense relief that I am not attached in that way to anyone. For so much of my life I was, but now I am free of passion, I see that it is a great blessing not to be in its thrall" (1987: 109). Sarton does, however, have some concern about young women deciding to live a life of solitude before they are emotionally ready and capable of handling its stresses, a concern that she expresses throughout her several journals.

I understand her concern, but all the same feel I'm ready to take the difficult step of embarking on this journey. I think I'm wise enough to know that I need to do this—that to live alone with my spirit is what needs to be done at this stage of my life, however young I may be. The one friend who is aware of my decision has told me that she sees my life as a waste of what it could be. This may well be true, but when I reach a fork in a road, I must make a choice as to which way to go and damn the consequences. This I have done.

In some ways, choosing to live a celibate life can be a controversial decision. Celibacy has often been considered to be a sellout to the authoritarian influence of whatever church one might belong to, especially if you're Catholic—as I try to be. Celibacy among priests and religious is a hot issue in the Catholic Church, with a number of people pushing for the ordination of married priests and for the relaxation of the rules against sexual activity on the part of priests and nuns, in order to encourage more vocations among those who might not feel they could handle a life of celibacy. Having been an active supporter of this struggle, I can well understand how my own choice of celibacy can be considered by some to be a betrayal of the cause.

In addition, if one is homosexual, choosing to live as a celibate can also be seen as a betrayal of the fight for acceptance of the ordination of gays and lesbians as ministers and priests—particularly if they wish to remain in a committed relationship. In past years a number of ordained homosexuals who have become involved in committed relationships have been ousted from their ministries for refusing to end those relationships—even if these relationships were regarded as marriages to the persons involved. Most denominations refuse to ordain sexually active gays and lesbians, and so if one is gay, to some people choosing celibacy seems like selling out to the conservative status quo.

As such, choosing celibacy can be a politically charged decision as well as purely a personal one. At the same time, it has spiritual ramifications, since some cultures and religious traditions believe that to have the most spiritually satisfying practice one should ideally be celibate. For example, Buddhist monks and nuns take vows of celibacy in order to free themselves of attachments that might keep them from attaining enlightenment, and we are of course aware of Catholic strictures against marriage for its professional religious for the same reason.

According to the book *Women of Spirit: Female Leadership in the Jewish and Christian Traditions*, by Eleanor McLaughlin and Rosemary Radford Ruether, a celibate life becomes a recognition and even a celebration of androgyny in a symbolic sense, in which the person "overcomes sexual dualism and experiences the reunion of maleness and femaleness in him/herself and in God. A spiritually androgynous self rises above the sexual dualism of physical bisexuality, an idea found in gnosticism and again among the Shakers" (24).

In my own situation, I find that celibacy has enhanced my spirituality in the sense that I no longer feel constricted by strict, scheduled religious activity nor by feeling silly for doing the things that I find most comfortable in my worship practices. Being a normally reticent person, I find it difficult to speak about my spirituality with most people, and in relationships over the years where I have gone to religious services with my partner, have felt self-conscious about seeming too ardent about my faith.

Choosing to be celibate and spiritual allows me to devote more time to following my religious practice in a way and at times in which I feel comfortable without being concerned that I am taking time away from a partner. The time that I find freed by not being committed to a partner is filled with an intense spirituality and with service to others that I might not otherwise have begun.

This is not to say that living a celibate life is a cakewalk. It's not. I do feel sometimes as if I am too much alone and do long for someone with whom to share my life. The pressure placed on single people to become part of a couple can be unbearable at times. Being celibate does not erase one's ability to love another, something I know full well since there is a person whom I do love, a "particular friend," to use an old phrase. And there is an ache in my heart when I see a couple obviously in love and content with each other that does tear at my soul when I least expect it. Yet such pain is almost a blessing, since it brings home the fact that I have made a sacrifice for the sake of something more, and so I must endeavor to make continuing with it worth the struggle.

I have found it helpful to think of my celibacy as a form of discipleship in the manner of Benedict Groeschel, who writes:

The awareness of discipleship is a great help to a person because it gives a purpose and goal to the price of singleness. One's self-respect and consequently, one's ability to be a blessing to others will be greatly enhanced by a firm commitment to discipleship. A clear intellectual understanding of unconscious motivation will serve to strengthen that commitment [to a chaste, single life]. (27)

I recognize that few things which are worthwhile come without paying a price of some kind and the benefits sometimes outweigh the pain. I have noticed that my occasional loneliness and longing for human contact has sensitized me to the pain felt by those who have become alone through no choice of their own. It has taught me to listen to their sorrows and to hear their suffering, perhaps offering some comfort along the way. I would like to think that I have helped someone through my understanding of my own struggle with being a woman alone.

Choosing a life of celibacy is far more than giving up sexual activity. As McLaughlin and Ruether say in *Women of Spirit*, celibacy traditionally "mandated the creation of a separate space for women" (24). Creating a separate space for myself has become an enforced awareness of my essential aloneness in the world. It is said that we enter this world alone and we leave it alone. But being alone doesn't necessarily mean that one is always lonely, something that I have learned, although it does add a keen, sharp edge to my solitude. Choosing a life alone is my affirmation that I can best serve my needs and the needs of those around me as a single, celibate person. At this point I do not care what others think of my chosen life-style. My decision is solely my responsibility—I will face the consequences and enjoy whatever benefits that may arise.

III *Discovery as the Gift of Age*

Women, and particularly older women, have historically suffered from the dualisms created by patriarchy—men over women, young over old. These dualistic images of the "other" are challenged in this section by three strong voices. As so many older persons do, these women reinterpret and reclaim the creative legacies of their past lives as they weave new patterns of meaning into their later years.

Widowed at fifty-nine, Roberta Way-Clark started her Second Life and asserts, more than ten years later, that it's never too late to grow.

In "Living Creatively," ever-single Betty Hares describes how retirement surprised her with a rekindled desire to have children, satisfied through the creativity of painting and poetry.

Divorced in her late fifties, Gloria Grover decided on celibacy in order to have more energy for personal and social change.

8   My Second Life: Single Again!

Roberta Way-Clark

> The words I hear are strength, laughter, endurance. Old woman I meet
> you deep inside myself.
>
> May Sarton, *Letters from Maine: New Poems*

What a slow and painful process it has been for me to pull my thoughts
together just to write this chapter. What a complex load I haul behind me
as I have come to live to this age. I am overwhelmed by the intensity of
my feelings, making it difficult for me, an old crone who has made it into
her seventies, to write about her Second Life.

This chapter is what I've managed to pull together. It's about my
personal journey, yes, but it's also about taking risks and it's certainly
about being single. It's about the journey many old women take as they
enter what I choose to call the Second Life. It's a reflection on the roles I
have taken over the years—wife, mother, employee, and keeper of the
house—but that I no longer take.

Indeed, as for many women like me, my personal journey has taken me
to a time of transitions—transitions that are often traumatic—when death,
divorce, desertion, illness, empty nest, or retirement obliterate our former
roles. What women like myself do with the years that are left determines
whether we will continue to grow or will retreat into sadness, sorrow, or
loneliness.

Transitions are powerful and, quite often, they are crises. The Chinese,
however, have a wonderful way of defining crisis. They call it a "dangerous opportunity." Now think about that for a moment. . . . Dangerous, yes;
a time for change, certainly . . . but an opportunity to make positive
changes in our lives, to change our perspective on life.

How do I feel about being single? I was married for forty years and I've been single for ten. Single is better. I revel in my singleness. I treasure it. Every morning I awake aware that, this day, I need only please myself. This may sound selfish, but it isn't. The fact that it pleases me to serve womankind (especially old women) is irrelevant, because I *choose* to do so and there's no one on which I must wait. Even though there can be great pleasure in cooking a meal for someone you love and in other ways serving as handmaiden, I know full well, as we all do, that these services are trivial at best, that almost anyone can perform them and that they amount to little in the long run.

As a single person, I have the energy to advocate for other older people and, I hope, make a small difference in our lives. I find it imprisoning even to contemplate another close relationship in which I would, because of gender, be forced again into a subservient role. I can't imagine wasting this precious energy darning socks and cleaning windows.

As older women, our choices in a "new" companion become fewer with every year we age, yet this is when we become more choosy. Recently, someone rhetorically asked me, "Isn't it any port in a storm?" My answer is no, that's not the way it is. I'm looking for a prince, but there are a lot of frogs out there.

You may be wondering if I'm lonely. In all honesty I must say that ever since my stray dog found me I've not known a lonely day. I've become her willing servant. There's maybe some truth in the saying, "A good dog is better than a poor husband." Now this isn't to say that I don't enjoy the company of men. In fact, I adore male energy and revel in the men I know and admire. But if I meet them as friends, then I meet them as equals, and I find great joy in that kind of relationship.

How did I get to this mind-set? The truth is that I was a feminist long before I knew the word. I've always fought against the restrictions of being female, just as I now fight the restrictions of being old. My quest has always been a complex and profound struggle as I fought for a sense of identity, importance, and power. But our patriarchal society has often viewed power in a woman as deviant and dangerous, so why did I persist at seeking this power? To explain, I must go back to my former life.

I married at twenty-one. It was wartime and it seemed so romantic to marry a serviceman who had been posted overseas. I left nurses' training just a few months before receiving my diploma, for after all, this was 1942 and I would never have to work again. What a joke that was! Indeed, by leaving before getting my R.N., I did, as it were, "shoot myself in the foot."

It wasn't long before I realized that I would have to work outside the home. Of course, my lack of education made it difficult for me to find work, let alone work that paid well. Remember that I was job hunting when pay equity and gender parity were unheard of. What made me angry was to work in an office with incompetent men who made twice my salary. I didn't challenge the logic of it, however; that was the way it was. After all, wasn't I lucky to *have* a job and to be keeping it from a single person? But my inner voice, still small then, would ask, "Aren't you putting groceries on the table just as these men are?"

Of course I was. My husband had early symptoms of Alzheimer's disease at a time when the public hadn't even heard of the disease. Years before doctors diagnosed my husband as having Alzheimer's, I knew that something dreadful and frightening was happening to him, but it was only after many years that a doctor finally told me that his state could only worsen. Even I, a trained nurse busy working as a bookkeeper, a nurse, a receptionist—anything!—had never heard of Alzheimer's disease.

Still, there was never enough money, so the bills kept piling up. When my two beloved daughters were in their teens, my husband's health forced him to declare bankruptcy, and we lost everything—even some money my parents had left me. Everything except our home. Talk about bitterness . . .

Talk about fear, too, as bank managers called *me* to demand payments. I wasn't the responsible party, but I was the one they harassed. The future looked bleak indeed. I remember sitting late one night, thinking about my options. That's when I wrote on a scrap of paper, almost matter-of-factly, "There's nowhere to go but up." Even as I write this and remember, my eyes burn and fill with tears. The hopeless, helpless agony of those days can still move me today.

I had always dabbled in painting and weaving, so with some encouragement from friends, I opened a shop in my living room. My rural location wasn't my choice but at that point, I hadn't read any books on starting a business. When I did, I discovered that the first four points to assess are location, location, location, and location! Despite the odds, however, the tourists and the local trade found me. By the second year, with more courage than brains or money, I built an addition to my home, and thus the Cottage Studio was born. Heavens, I had become an entrepreneur! As Mark Twain said, "All you need in this life is ignorance and confidence and then success is sure."

So at fifty I became a shopkeeper, an independent craftswoman, despite severe vertigo and arthritis that required me to use a cane and a neck brace. (Remember my mentioning risk taking? This is what I meant.) It was nothing for me to work eighteen hours a day, day after day. I often rose at five o'clock to paint in the kitchen or to weave in the den. Many times I painted a picture in the morning and sold it in the evening, with many warnings not to touch it.

Did I have talent? I don't think so. I painted hundreds of lighthouses and even more fish shacks. . . . No, not talent, but a little skill that I exploited to the hilt. There was also the total and terrifying financial insecurity I felt, which, without a doubt, brought forth my skill and talent as a shopkeeper. I did have an unexpected gift for selling, so I muse that in a former life I must have been a horse trader. Had I had economic security, I never would have dredged up these skills and talents, but faced with the possibility of welfare, I knew I had to make the Cottage Studio a success. As someone said, "Serendipity or, if you will, the hand of God" was at work here.

Is it true that "creativity is the other face of adversity?" I think so. Many women I've known have blossomed after a hard life, but it's also true that a hard life has destroyed other women. So women are made stronger by adversity *if* they survive. I think that what saved me (aside from luck) was my upbringing, which taught me to take risks and to think that I would succeed in whatever I undertook. Those ten years I spent in business were hard, but they were successful and exciting. From the onset I saw that I could make a good living this way, but through those years I never lost my sense of wonder. Every night, as I closed up the Cottage Studio, I would turn around and say to my little shop, "Good night and thank you."

Because of my disastrous marriage and the menial jobs I was forced to take before I opened my shop, I felt a great loss of status and became determined to upgrade my education—a risky proposition in those days in Cape Breton. However, again I was lucky. Brought up the only child of aging parents, I had a father who was involved in politics and the co-op movement, which was powerful at that time. From both my parents I inherited good self-esteem and learned the value of education, so even though I didn't do it at the "right" time, I started taking university-level courses shortly after I opened the Cottage Studio.

I started with night classes in accounting—not because I was particularly interested in the subject, but because that's all that was available. I was part of a large class with only two women. I was convinced that everyone there knew more than I did (certainly they were all younger) but, wouldn't you know it, when the teacher posted the first marks, the other woman ranked first and I ranked second. This in our patriarchal society! Then I took correspondence courses from Mount Allison University—the most lonely and difficult way to study. I obtained a few credits, but as the shop expanded and required more of my time and energy, I could no longer continue working on my education.

However, after running the shop for ten years, I could see that the times were changing. People didn't have as much ready cash; oil prices were going up, and all over the province, craft shops and fairs were springing up. I had had little competition when I started, so my timing had been right, if not my location. But the time had come for me to go out of business, so I did.

My husband died the following year.

It was my turn now. My Second Life was beginning.

With much fear, I approached Mount Saint Vincent University, a university renowned for its support of women. I kept asking the same questions. "Am I too old to learn? Will you take me at this age—fifty-nine?" Suddenly, all the confidence I had built up over my shop years seemed to evaporate, and it was with great surprise that I found myself again in inner turmoil. But Dr. Mairi Macdonald, the Director of Continuing Education at the time, reassured me: "Of course you can come! We're delighted to have you." With her warmth and encouragement, she became my mentor and friend and remains so to this day.

I was allowed credit for all my former work, even my two and a half years of nurses' training. I was thus able to complete an undergraduate degree and obtain a diploma in gerontology in three years—three years of growth, I assure you.

Coming from a village to a city was traumatic in itself. I used to drive miles on the Bedford Highway (where the "Mount" is located) to buy groceries. When questioned about this odd habit, I had to admit that I couldn't find my way if I strayed from the highway.

The first year, I accepted the donship at my residence and was in charge of 150 young women. They learned from me and I from them . . . and some things I learned only years later. For instance, I found out that they used to hide beer in the fridge by wrapping it in brown paper on which they marked "hamburger," an ingenious subterfuge, given that I don't eat meat. In another instance, one of my former residents recently asked me if I remembered the night I was driving them home from downtown when a few young men were following us, honking their horn. I did. I even remembered that I was laughing as I waved to them. What I didn't know, this young woman finally told me: "Joan was mooning them out the back window of your station wagon." Isn't higher education wonderful?

I was one of the very few older people on campus in those days, and certainly the only one to live in residence. The culture shock was extreme. Once I innocently went to class in an ultrasuede suit, but I soon learned to dress more casually. I was continually taken for a sister at this Catholic university, many times for a professor, and occasionally for the president, who was about my age. (I still wonder if someone has ever mistaken her for me.) Having a fifty-nine-year-old student must have been both a threat and a challenge to some of the young professors just starting to make their mark in academia. I may have even lost marks for being mistaken for the professor, who was thus ignored by the students.

I'm pleased to note that ten years after my first year there are many grey heads on campus. Back then I felt alone in this strange new world, which I had entered as a successful businesswoman but where I quickly became another student—but an older student. I found myself in an unfamiliar culture in which I knew neither the rules nor the questions to ask. I had left behind all that was familiar to me, my roots, whereas other mature students had homes to go to after class where they could get support and encouragement.

That first year was devastating in its loneliness, as I was also going through a rough grieving process for my husband. This surprised me, for he had been ill for so long that I had thought the grief would be minimal. But it wasn't so. If I could have wished him back, with all his deficiencies, I would have done so. It was only later, when studying the grieving process in my Death and Dying class, that I realized my reactions were normal.

After my undergraduate work, I decided that I wanted to complete a master's degree, so I applied to another university. I was accepted, but with a coldness that I couldn't have borne if I hadn't had the supportive experience of the Mount. I certainly couldn't have started my undergraduate work at this other university. But I worked hard and graduated two years later with a master's in Adult Education.

Then came the final step: I put together a committee, wrote a proposal and began the Ph.D. program. Six months into the program, however, I was turned down. What I have in writing is a letter stating that the committee could find nothing in my background that would lead it to think that I could obtain a Ph.D. Rubbish, of course . . . but that's another story.

I was now an "older" woman, and I was becoming aware of the prejudices our society holds against the elderly, especially older women. It was a great shock to have a young man one day roll down his car window and shout, "Get off the road, you stupid old bitch!" Good heavens, I thought, he means *me*! In some unknown way, *I* had offended him. Was I going too slow? Was it that I threatened him with my "oldness"? Did he want to get rid of me, in some kind of twisted belief that the same thing would therefore not happen to him? Who knows, but it's shattering to realize that you have grown old and stupid overnight—at least in this young man's eyes.

It's interesting that we can be racist, if you will, because we'll never change our race or color. We can be sexist, if we like, because we'll not likely change our sex. But if we're ageist, we work against ourselves, for barring a young death (which isn't great either), we will become old. It behooves us, therefore, to stamp out these stereotypes against the elderly. I think the baby boomers, with their great numbers and power, will take care of this sad situation, but that too is another story.

Here's another thought on this aging business. I firmly believe that we are all stuck internally at an age that doesn't necessarily correlate with our chronological age. I know that mine is thirty-six, and the only way I know that I'm an aging person is when I get feedback that tells me so. I have many stories to illustrate this, but I think the best one is when someone tells me, with definite amazement, "You're still working! Well, good for you!" (Now isn't that a backhanded compliment if you ever heard one?) Obviously I can't solve this problem alone, so this is a call to arms for all older women and men to join the fight against the stereotypes our society ascribes to the aging. As I feel the lack of energy from the accumulated years, I wonder if I have the strength, and yet . . . *and yet* . . . I'm only thirty-six!

Because of the role change I went through in becoming a widow, I took the risk of changing my whole lifestyle. Perhaps it would have been easier for me to have stayed at home and vegetated or, perhaps, to have remarried and resumed my former role. But no. Instead, I thought to myself, "I still have ten good years left, and I intend to make the most of them." Well, what do you know! It's ten years later and I still have another ten good years left. Well, maybe five . . .

During the first ten years of my Second Life, I have become aware of the value of women friends. When I was part of a couple, struggling to work and care for my two daughters, there seemed to be little time or energy to nurture the deep friendships I've formed in these later years— friendships that, for me, have become a great source of strength and love. The friendships I had in my former life certainly weren't as rich as those I have now, for, like Sarton, I can share "strength, laughter, endurance" with these women.

I also found that as I aged, I've made friends with younger women, women who value me. These friendships have become important to me as I continue to live in a society that I feel devalues me and, indeed, sometimes makes me invisible because of my age. Is it because I dared to invade the milieu of the young? Why does this happen, I wonder? Is it because younger people can't bear to look upon wrinkles, grey hair, a stooped stance, and swollen ankles? Don't the young see the beauty of old age, or do they only see the ugliness? "Not me," they say. "I'll never be like that." Yet the fear remains with them—the fear that they might. I want so much to tell them, "What you see is not what I am! I'm only thirty-six!"

Are friendships really deeper and richer when we are older? Yes, I most certainly think they are. For one thing, our own self-actualizing process is better developed, our working days are mostly over, and often we have been left alone by death or desertion. I also believe that we're in the stage in life when we can support and empower each other and accompany our sisters on the last part of our journey. Granted, I may be wrong in thinking that this comfort comes only in late life, because Leah Cohen says in *Small Expectations*, "Women who have never uttered a feminist word in their lives seemed to appreciate that female friendship was perhaps the most sustaining aspect of their lives. As many said, it was only with other women that they felt valued and taken seriously" (205). Are we to think, then, that some women are fortunate enough to find this support early in life, while others, like myself, find it only later?

What I do know is that I find great joy and comfort as we laugh together, plan together, grieve together, and, yes, even rage at old age together. I'm continually amazed at these women's intelligence, beauty, goodness, and fundamental courage. They are women of substance and integrity. The friends of my youth are mostly forgotten, so why would I not love these seasoned, substantial, and supportive companions of my old age? Their friendship is precious and sacred to me. These women are my tribe. Lord, let me die with one friend left!

But back to the present. . . . The stress-related illnesses resulting from my first life are now very manageable. I'm fortunate to have an interesting job as the director of the Care for the Caregiver program at Mount Saint Vincent University. My contract ends in the spring of 1992. Since I'm now seventy, it may be time to retire—at least from full-time work. We shall see.

It's been and still is a glorious Second Life. I wish the same for all older women and men. The risk is worth taking, even though I must admit that this new world was scary at times. As I stare into my past, however, I can see that I needed to be single in order to change and grow. There's no doubt that through all the struggles of my first life, I had this feeling of having lost a part of myself, and all the work I've done since then has been to find that missing part. There's no doubt: I needed to be alone, not lonely but in solitude. I see myself withdrawing: I need the silence. How remarkable that I never guessed that this was the way to my happiness, that only through living alone could I reach fulfillment.

Life itself is, I think, this long, painful progression of growth toward the essence. A. H. Maslow and others have named the growth that takes place in later years "self-actualization." I agree that this is our main task in later life, but of necessity, this growth must be inward. It must also lead away from the intellectual and toward the spiritual. I'm not talking about religion, but the linking of all human life. No, scratch that! The linking of all life: animals, plants, the environment. This is the growth of the mystic. In my mind, what's inherent in this growth is finding the part of myself that was forgotten in my years as half of a couple. Of course, all is not sunshine; there are still dark periods when I wish to end the struggle or go for the frivolous, to stop this painful work of self and learn to play. But something keeps me from doing this, so I'm stuck with the continual exploration of the "why."

Yes, my Second Life has been exciting, rewarding, satisfying and, I hope, of some significance. Being single has allowed me the time and energy to seek fulfillment in my personal journey. It has also allowed me to encourage other women, so it's true that we are able to empower each other. Let's hold out our hands, therefore, to our sisters and inspire them to take the risk necessary for their Second Lives.

As I contemplate retirement, I feel a strange excitement, a sense of freedom. My still, small voice says, "Now you can do what you were destined to do. What a slow learner you were not to realize that your destiny lies in _____ ." Indeed, those last words are still hidden from me.

But who knows? Perhaps I have another ten good years. After all, I'm only thirty-six.

9 Living Creatively

Betty Hares

> But when we have discovered that a necessity is really necessary, that
> it is unalterable and we can do nothing to avert or change it, then our
> freedom consists in the acceptance of the inevitable as the medium of
> our creativity.
>
> H. A. Williams, *Tensions*

Married people remember, vividly, the day they decided to marry. I
remember the day I knew I would remain single as clearly as if it were
only yesterday. I had finished my nurse training toward the end of World
War II and was standing at the foot of the staircase in the Nurses' Home
talking to a friend. Suddenly I said, "I have a feeling I shall never marry!"
It was a shattering intuition that seemed to receive confirmation some days
later, when the landlady in the house where I was lodging said jokingly,
"You're not the marrying kind, love!" I don't think it had ever occurred to
me that the vocation I had chosen to follow would include being single.
Now I knew in my bones that it would. It was no use going on hoping that
I would marry; that would have led to bitterness and frustration. Nothing
in my experience so far had given me any real hope of marriage. I had had
a few male friends, but these friendships never blossomed into mutual
love, and the only person who wanted to marry me, I could not accept. So
I had to accept the probability and shape my life accordingly.

I decided that life could still be full and satisfying, and that decision has
proved right, not in any glib or easy way, for being single is as difficult as
being married, I am sure. It has to be worked at, pondered, molded, shaped,
and reshaped like a ball of clay before any kind of image is produced.
Acceptance of singleness has not been a once-for-all act, but more a

succession of acts, in rather the same way as conversion is often a process rather than a "Damascus road" experience. It is a creative process which for me is still going on, sometimes, oh, so slowly! New situations and new challenges demand a rededication if there is to be a real release of creative energy.

My acceptance of singleness at that point, upon completion of my nurse training, gave me the liberty to respond to an urge that had haunted me since childhood: to be a missionary. I had not always cherished that urge. For several years it was an irritant from which I did my best to escape, but it never left me entirely. Now I was free. While my friends were putting homes together and getting married and having children, I could choose, without hindrance, to do what I wanted to do and felt constrained to do—assuming, of course, that I would be accepted by the Methodist Missionary Society. My parents were well and ready to accept whatever the future held for me. I offered and was accepted, and so began an incredible journey that took me all over the world—a journey to openness of mind and spirit, the story of which I have told in my book *Journeying into Openness*.

For a long time, being single did not worry me at all, or impinge greatly on my thinking or being. It is not difficult to see why. Amid all the busyness and fascination of being a missionary with the Methodist Church, there was little time for introspection or regret. First of all I worked in China at the time of its "liberation," and then in Ghana, West Africa, sharing as far as possible in the joys and pains of that delightful country and her people during the change from British control to independence. Male and female colleagues, both Ghanaian and Western, were warm and close, as they continued to be when I returned to England to become a secretary in the Overseas Division of the Methodist Church. There were times when those of us who lived alone said laughingly that we wished we had a spouse to do our packing, cleaning, and washing for us as our male colleagues had. But for the most part, I cherished my independence and my freedom to travel and organize my life as I wished. Closing the front door of my flat behind me after a busy day in the office was a wonderful feeling. Being able to prepare talks and reports without the interruptions and demands of a family was a blessing.

So it came as something of a surprise to find when I retired that there were still lingering regrets about not having married and especially about not having a family. I had lived a full and creative life, perhaps more full and more creative than it would have been had I had a husband and children. My house had been open to all. I had been free to travel the world. Books, music, poetry, friends, and so much more had been mine. So why did I feel this renewed sense of loss? Retirement can be something of a wilderness. Suddenly there was too much space, too little company, too much aloneness, too little chatter and noise.

There was no one to touch, no one to throw my arms around, no one to share how I felt. Later on, when life once more became full and creative, though in different ways, I wrote a poem about my feelings.

Wilderness

Place of withdrawal
 Spirit
 God within
willing extraction
from the world
pressing
round the rim
of isolation
 giving meaning
 asking questions
 demanding answers.

Place of stripping
 Spirit
 God within
sand lashing wind
stinging face
and heart
whipping
round the dunes
of desolation
 baring self-deceit
 cleansing vision
 scouring pride.

Place of exposure
 Spirit
 God within
scattering security
in emptiness
removing
signposts to certainty

feeling bare
standing alone
setting free.

Place of glory
    Spirit
    God within
sun-blazing light
illuminating
depths of darkness
surprising
the landscape of living
with rainbows
        stimulating hope
        showing direction
        strengthening resolve.

Because, of course, God's spirit goes on working in our singleness, our aloneness (and we are all single in the end), and brings to birth things of which we never dreamed, if we trust the desolation of the wilderness. And She does it in all kinds of ways and through all kinds of people, through our memories and through our conscious or hidden talents—gifts we had never acknowledged, perhaps, "children" never cherished.

Retirement brought me to another frontier of acceptance of my singleness, the crossing of which would be both more demanding and more rewarding and creative than at the start of my career.

Freedom is something to be cherished, and for the single person, it is a very special gift, but because it is, it is also a great responsibility, as all gifts are. The single person living alone does not have the restraints of a close family to act as a curb upon desires and choices and to help by asking questions and probing motives. It becomes easy to live for oneself: selfish choices are more easily hidden, and doubtful motives go unchallenged. I am still learning the importance of having friends and colleagues who perform these services for me. If freedom is to be used creatively, it can never be unrestrained freedom; it has to be related to the freedom of others and molded in both receiving and giving loving service. For the married person or the single person living with others, those boundaries are immediate. For the single person living alone, they have to be quite deliberately sought and delineated.

Working with the church overseas, first of all as a nurse in China and then as the principal of a women's (lay) training center in Ghana, provided me with boundaries within which to exercise my freedom and to learn how to use it. In "retirement" I had to define new boundaries. I was free to choose in a way I had never been before. On the other hand, the physical boundaries of my home loomed large, for the simple reason that I spent more time within them than I had when I was commuting to London every day.

I began to realize the importance of creating a real home and not simply a pied-à-terre, a place where my friends, married or single, could relax and feel at home; where there are pictures and music, my paints and books lying around, all the signs of living. I was leading a discussion on singleness once and said in the course of introducing the subject that married people were often more ready to invite single people into their homes "to become one of the family" than they were to accept the hospitality of their single friends. One young married woman in the group who had two small children said that she would not feel at home where there were no muddles, no children's toys scattered about. She had a point. The clinically tidy bachelor flat, which is only a place to sleep and eat between the real business of living done elsewhere, or the house-proud flat without a thing out of place is not an attractive home. I have enjoyed making a real home in which I live and into which others enjoy coming, a place where I and my friends can be at peace. I am, I say, a "one-person family" in a "one-person family home."

Nevertheless, I have learned too that trying to live creatively as a single person requires that I join groups in which discussion stimulates new thinking and new skills are learned to share with other groups that may create new forms of community that challenge the exclusiveness of the Western "nuclear family" and in which women and men are free to create friendships without the fear and suspicion single people, particularly single women, seem to generate. But creative singleness requires, too, that I do not confine my friendships to other singles as I have been tempted to do, fearing that I would be absorbed into someone else's family or looked upon as a surrogate auntie or baby minder. Maintaining friendships with married people is not easy. They have different priorities, different commitments, but that is not a good reason for keeping away from them.

I have learned not to believe those who say that real friendship between marrieds and singles is not possible. It is not only possible but enriching, providing that each accepts the other as he or she is and tries to understand the different life-style the other needs to create in order to be true to the self within. Acceptance is the key to creative friendship and a creative life-style.

It is important to me that I have young friends as well as those of my own age. Single people who are not surrounded by a growing family are deprived of the freshness and vitality of the young, their sense of excitement and their ability to look forward. It is easy as one grows older to become set in one's ways, not to move on, not to maintain an open mind, to be afraid of a bit of untidiness.

It was, therefore, a great bonus when I retired and moved from London to my home city of Bristol to be asked to teach part-time at the Methodist Theological College about one and a half miles away from where I live. This not only provides me with an anchor and a discipline (very important for singles) but keeps me on my toes mentally and spiritually. I have to keep up with what is going on in the world if I am to teach World Affairs with any meaning, and I have to be prepared for some pretty sharp theological questions at times. But perhaps more than that, the group of first-year students I am involved with (not all young, of course, but younger than I am) provides me with the stimulus I need as a single person to explore new ideas with others, and to share in their creativity.

Singleness and not having children are not, of course, to be equated, in the same way as being married and having children are not. There are today many people who choose to have children and remain single, but for me that was not an option. Children need more than one parent. Moreover, for a Christian, having a child depends upon having a real relationship of love with someone who is not committed to anyone else. I cannot believe in promiscuity for the sake of bearing children. But that has not made the acceptance of childlessness any easier for me. It has always been my greatest regret and, perhaps, the hardest thing I have had to come to terms with. Yet what Harry Williams has written in his book *Tensions* is so true: "But when we have discovered that a necessity is really necessary, that it is unalterable and we can do nothing to avert or change it, then our freedom consists in the acceptance of the inevitable as the medium of our creativity" (1976, 105).

For me, accepting the necessity of childlessness has created a flow of creative energy through painting and poetry. My pictures and my poems have become my children. Giving birth to them is sometimes easy, sometimes painful, but always joyful:

> Sometimes I feel
> the me in me
> struggling to be free,
> a hand, a toe, a limb
> probing from within.

Why is this pregnancy so long?
Why am I slow in being born?

Parting with my pictures is as difficult as saying "good-bye" to a son or daughter and as joyful as knowing that they are giving pleasure to others. But I like to know where they are, who has bought or been given the painting, and who has used my poems.

I have always been able to write and known that I could paint. That I did not choose, for many years, to bear these children was my loss. The sad fact is that I was too busy. Discovering that I was still capable of doing so rather late in life has been a great delight.

I started to paint again during the five years before retirement from work with the Methodist Overseas Division. In my book *Journeying into Openness*, I have told how one day in 1976, while in Bristol Cathedral, my sister picked up a leaflet advertising a painting retreat that was to be held at Llangasty in Breconshire, Mid-Wales, and sent it to me on the off chance that I might be interested. I wrote asking if they would accept a mere Methodist (the organizers were Anglican). They would and I went. It was one of those gloriously timeless weeks, and we spent most of it out of doors in the warm sunshine. In the beautiful and peaceful countryside around Lake Llangorse and the Brecon Beacons, we painted, walked, or just sat; we listened to music and discovered silence. It revived in me the desire to paint as a regular activity. I bought some new materials and set out on a new journey.

Retirement provided me with the time and opportunity to paint more seriously, and later on, under the guidance of a Bristol watercolorist, quite a lot of progress was made, I like to think.

Painting needs observation and attention. It developed in me the need to find stillness, and it made me aware of the communication taking place between me and the "otherness" of things and people. They communed with me and I with them in a new way. I discovered that I was not alone. I began to see into things; there were colors and shapes, lights and shades I had never noticed before.

As I wrote earlier,

We are all creative beings made in the image of our creator God. The trouble with most of us is that our creativity is inhibited by "experts", and by our own lack of trust in ourselves. We are constantly comparing our efforts with those of others, fearful that they are looking over our shoulders at what we are doing. We want to learn "the rules". Discovering the creativity within us, the intuitive side of our nature, is to do with finding the freedom of spirit to create what is uniquely ours, that which expresses *our* truth. (Hares, 141)

Accepting who we are and what we cannot change enables us to discover, if we will, the depths of creativity within us, releasing that which we did not know we possessed, leading us, married or single, to that fullness of humanity that is our God-given right.

10 Single Connectedness

Gloria W. Grover

When twenty-seven years of marriage came to an end for me, it was necessary—painfully—to learn to say "I" again instead of "we." Memories, anecdotes, stories that had always been first person plural now became first person singular. There was no more "we." That was sixteen years ago.

I tend to think of my marital condition now as singular rather than single. I am a mother and grandmother who is first of all an "I": a person, human being, individual, whose identity far exceeds her biological and legal relationships. I am Ms., not Mrs. or Miss. I always introduce myself by my first name; my children, grandchildren, friends—young and old—call me Gloria. I like my first name, which was given to me by my mother, and I resent the fact that "maiden" name and "married" name are those of father and spouse. Had I thought it through sixteen years ago, I probably would have baptized myself with a new last name, but I didn't, so I use my first name alone as much as possible.

Becoming an "I" again has taken time. Singlehood has given me the opportunity to separate role from function, identity from role. Sometimes it's a little frightening. Because I'm no longer a wage earner, I have no fixed economic or professional role anymore, either. I do not have structures into which I fit and into which I am absorbed. So the question of identity (who am I? why am I?) surfaces continually.

Answering—or rather exploring—these questions is appropriate at any time of life. It's perhaps most necessary as I approach the end of my lifespan at seventy-three. It's much easier, I find, to deal with ultimate questions of reality and meaning as a single person who sets her own agenda, who is not distracted by another's agenda, needs, demands.

Marriage (or partnership) requires a heavy mutual investment in comforting but often trivial routines, an investment of self in interactions of all sorts that tend to lock one into a closed system: an exclusive intimacy that is physical, mental, moral, verbal.

It amazed me to discover how much energy became available to me to explore new approaches to life after my marriage ended and the initial shock and pain wore off. Nearing sixty, I was able to enter a seminary and complete a three-year ministry program. I was able to find definitions of ministry that suited my own ideas about new forms of community, worship, ritual, prayer, relationships. These—along with writing—formed a framework for daily discipline that underlay my adaptation to aloneness and singleness.

A good deal of my wonderful new energy was generated by experiences in the women's movement, which was then moving us all in new directions. The excitement of the women's liberation movement at that time was incredible. Suddenly we questioned everything. We challenged ourselves constantly. Our women friends were our sisters, daughters, mentors. As we slowly separated ourselves from our ancient roles of handmaidens and comforters, we found that it was our women friends who inspired and sustained us.

Friendship and love are not distinct. For me, friendship is love without significant elements of possessiveness or eroticism. I found that my women friends (and a very few men friends) gave me love in a more satisfying way than husbands, lovers. To ensure that friendship would not give way to possessive eroticism, I adopted celibacy as a way of life. I wanted to be free to use my energy as I wished—an impossible goal when one is in a sexual partnership, in my experience.

So for a period of about twelve years I have been deeply involved in small groups of women (and one group that is open to men also) who are committed to feminist liberationist views of society, of relationships, of personal and social change. To spell that out, we understand that social, economic, and religious structures are rooted in patriarchy. We see that patriarchy exalts hierarchy, domination, and control by males and encourages rigid dualistic patterns of thinking, for example, arbitrary gender distinctions and roles, class and race distinctions into superior/inferior, body/mind and body/spirit oppositions, heaven/earth. The sad fact is that all of us are permeated by patriarchal values because that's how we were raised.

It has taken me a very long time to understand how, from the beginning, as a female I have been in abusive relationships with my childhood family (children have no rights), with my adult family (I was the handmaiden who always said yes), and with my church. I was a Roman Catholic. I do not mean to say that no good came of these experiences. One learns. I learned. And some of the family and church members learned too. And we can laugh together now about how it used to be.

When I woke up to my capacity—one most women have—for enduring abusive relationships, I realized I'd better stay single. And for two reasons: (1) I would avoid disappointment, (2) I would have more energy to use for personal and social change.

There are lonely times, of course. I'm an extrovert who needs people, and most of my life I've lived in partnerships. I'm always in danger of narcissism, of mood swings that come from lack of feedback, of getting cut off from reality. But I'm in touch with friends, grown daughters, and grandchildren. The hugs and kisses I get from children and adult friends are vital to my health and self-esteem. I try to keep in touch with myself through writing. I have time to write poetry, to listen to music, to walk, to think, to dream, to meditate in ways that are impossible unless one lives alone.

Solitude permits insights and growth. It obliges us to acknowledge the emptiness of our busyness and self-importance. It obliges us to acknowledge that in fact we are each alone in fundamental ways, that loneliness is a necessary condition of being human—of human consciousness. We *know* we are going to get old, to lose people and qualities that we value; we *know* we are going to die. We *know* that no matter how much we love someone else, we will remain separate persons.

I like living alone in spite of the lonely times. But my grandchildren and their parents (one parent at a time, as they are no longer together) are upstairs. Noises and sounds remind me constantly of their presence. I go off occasionally to an island for a retreat that entails being entirely alone—no upstairs people. I find this good for restoring my sense of relationship to the "all"—for cutting out the role-playing, getting back to fundamentals. In *Recovering: A Journal*, May Sarton says about fundamental life purpose: "The more our bodies fail us, the more naked and demanding is the spirit, the more open and loving we can become if we are not afraid of what we are and of what we feel" (138). Aloneness forces us to know who we are and what we feel. The end of the process is to be more open and more loving.

I read a lot, mostly women writers. For about ten years I've been devouring women's novels, stories, journals, and poetry to get a sense of what women are doing, thinking, writing, saying. Lessing, Rich, Atwood, Walker, Sarton, Laurence, and many others are spiritual guides for me, as well as friends, theologians, sociologists, historians, and prophets. I think

of Dante's great flower image in the "Paradiso"—a white rose composed
of tiers of angels and saints forming the petals. My flower is made up of
all these wonderful women—and Martha Graham, Nellie McClung,
Georgia O'Keefe, and so many other women whose spirits live. I have
been healed by these women. They mediate the divine for me, lift me
up.

Recently I participated in a healing ritual led by a native woman who
had recovered from a long period of alcoholism to return to her own tribal
spirituality. We were about thirty women representing many traditions
(Protestant and Catholic), ages, regions of Canada, stages of life. In the
ritual we were purified by sweet grass, connected with tobacco, and lifted
up with chanting. Mind, heart, body, and spirit were acknowledged,
symbolized, purified, and healed with words and silence, collective sharing, and individual meditation. What power there was in that ceremony!
What power there was in that native woman! What power there was in the
realization that moved in us that we had been victims of a brutal, death-
oriented mythology, the mythology of white male superiority. We had all
been tricked by that mythology into exalting mind (rational analytical
linear logic) at the expense of intuition, feeling, spirit, body, wholeness,
health.

The spirit moves where it will. Today it moves in women, natives,
blacks, marginal, and oppressed peoples. If I want to be part of this, I need
to be single and, to a certain extent, single-minded, which means being
celibate as well. To champion the victims, whether of poverty, abuse, or
discrimination (cultural, racial, sexual—against gays and lesbians) requires a certain freedom that rarely exists in marriage.

The freedom from economic constraint is vital, too. I am a pensioner
now; I don't have to work for a wage or salary, which is enormously
freeing.

All in all, I find this a fine period of life. I'm not physically able to do
as much as I'd like. I have to budget my energy as carefully as my money.
But I have more freedom, more friends, more joy, and less emotional pain
than when I was younger. I also have less certainty; all the old shibboleths
are gone. The notions about family, church, hereafter—all gone. In their
place are new insights, questions, tentatives—but no certainties.

I'll give you an example. After twelve years of marriage, my daughter
and her husband separated. They had four young children. We had bought
our house together. They were upstairs; I had a separate basement apartment. Their separation came as a terrible blow to me—another certainty
gone. Together we worked out a plan. My daughter and ex-son-in-law
move in and out of the house. Usually she is there four nights a week and

he is there three nights, but he stays longer some days to even out the time. Vacations are divided up for longer periods of time. Each is equally responsible for cooking, shopping, laundry, and cleaning, and all expenses are shared. They each have a place to live elsewhere (he is now in a common-law relationship). Their arrangements have been worked out in great detail with a mediator/counselor (no lawyers).

This unusual plan of joint custody and joint operation of our house has been working pretty well for about five years now, with family conferences when necessary. My former son-in-law's partner is accepted by all of us. My daughter plans not to marry again. We each have to adjust continually to their moving in and out (I tend to forget who is going to be there when), but it works. There's no certainty that it will work forever. But then, there are really no certainties in life. There never were, but for a long time I had illusions that there were. One is better off without illusions.

I know that the small groups I belong to (house church, women's spirituality, and justice-making and support groups) are fluid, changeable, and certainly mortal. But for now they enable me to find a community of searchers, questioners, other singular people who are not necessarily single.

It's a truism to say that we are living in an era of constant change, prolonged transition. It's a "meantime." I'm looking for wisdom that enables me to live in this meantime, to let each day bring its own truth.

The book of Proverbs tells us that Wisdom is out there—on the street corners, hilltops, calling us to eat her bread and drink her wine. She sends out her maidens, she shouts, she summons (Prov. 8–9).

Each day brings its bread and wine, its wisdom, its experience of the sacred, of the ordinary things that are sacred because all life is sacred. Each day *is* bread and wine—another taste of life, another experience, another adventure.

It's not easy to hold onto this sense of the sacredness of living when one is subject to another's moods, needs, and problems twenty-four hours a day. I am thankful for my singleness. When I fail to profit from it and enjoy it, then it's my fault alone, my responsibility. No one else can be blamed. And that, finally, is the greatest gift singlehood and celibacy have given me: I have been made responsible for my own life, for my own choices, growth, wisdom, or lack of. I don't feel trapped in compromise. I can't use someone else as an excuse for laziness, dishonesty, or fear; I can take risks.

Married people are rarely risk takers. Families tend to make us conservative (the mortgage, the job, the children's needs!). Love affairs—in my experience—tend to limit risk taking to the affair itself. I do not think significant personal and social change can take place without risk. The status quo is safe or seems to be; the known, however awful, seems less dangerous than the unknown, to most of us. Risk taking is at the heart of change for individuals and societies. It is easier for singles to take risks and to be intentional about it. They can be committed to process as well as goal: to new ways of thinking, being, or doing. If we are to have a more just society, we have to find just ways of living and of relating to others. As a single, I am obliged to work out relationships that have little to do with structures, because I'm not in most of the structures. That opens me up to important questions of justice and ethics, because I'm not provided with the easy answers already worked out by conventional structures.

Being old gives me a certain detachment about structures, too, and about roles, social conventions, and expectations. That kind of detachment, as well as my singlehood, frees me to be myself. My joints are often stiff, but my spirit is usually dancing.

The following poem which I wrote recently, sums up my sense that singleness can mean more, not less, connectedness.

The Universal Dance

Dance the earth
      cooking weeding
   playing with children cats
   walking swimming talking
   wearing your different hats
     citizen lover friend

Dance the cosmos
      star moon sun wind
        in music art

Dance the central act
      dance your beating heart
        in silence

Life that pulses blood that pushes
self that is can be danced only
in silent connectedness to the unspeakable
     whole

IV The Challenges of Career and Life-style

Single women often enjoy the freedom both to establish a career and to determine their own life-style. The authors in this section demonstrate that this freedom of choice involves responsibility and compassionate discernment, which is reciprocated by society.

In "The Single Journey as Vocation," Eileen O'Brien advocates recognition of being single as a vocation that ideally would have a structured period of discernment and that would be celebrated by a public commitment.

Jo Ellen Heil's "heart sings" when she is reclaiming women's herstory—which she has persisted at doing in spite of considerable obstacles.

Called to prophetic ministry, Pamela Ann Moeller has survived divorce but describes the pressure, professionally and personally, to compromise.

11 The Single Journey as Vocation

Eileen E. O'Brien

I am single. Not "not married" and not "not a religious sister." I am single as a positive state, as a choice for now. Currently I am discerning my vocation: I may very well feel God's call strongly enough to positively choose the single life and maybe even to vow myself to the single life. That is my journey.

Some people are single by circumstance—divorce, death of a spouse, laicization, separation from a religious community. Some are single by default. They never found the right mate or a suitable religious community to join and, since we are all born single, they just continue to be single.

There are also people among us who feel called by God to be single. It is not a case of not finding the right mate or not finding the right religious community. It is a call from God to the single life. Having "a call" used to refer to people discerning a vocation to religious life, yet it can refer to any of the vocations. God loves each one of us in a unique way. Each of us is called to answer God's love with her or his life. How can I best respond to God's love? How can I best spread God's love in my life and in others' lives? How can I best lead a loving life? How can I best live out my baptismal call to service? These are key questions.

These expanded views of vocation and call developed gradually for me with the grace of God and the help of friends. As a young adult, I looked into religious life. I had some striking role models from school and from my parish, and I wanted to follow them. These role models were sisters, priests, and brothers. I was attracted to their lives, their service, and their openness. Their vows of poverty, chastity, and obedience did not attract me. I saw them as necessary items I would have to take on to live that service-oriented and open life I desired.

There was an uneasiness in me for a few years as I struggled with this. I felt attracted to and repelled by the image of myself as a religious sister. (As a Catholic woman, brotherhood and ordained priesthood are closed to me.) The aversion was strengthened for me as I became more aware of the role of women in the institutional Catholic Church and of its limitations: how calls to the ordained priesthood are not affirmed and how many dedicated religious are, unfortunately, seen as "cheap labor." Could I put myself even deeper into such an institution? I felt like I was on the edge of a pool with people ready to push me in. "I'll jump in *when* I'm ready and *if* I'm ready. Don't push me!"

After graduation, my position again put me in contact with a community filled with vibrant, faithful, happy religious, and feelings—"Maybe this is for me"—arose again. This time, though, I looked deeper. I saw that what attracted me was service, not sisterhood. Sisterhood is a subset of service, just as married life and single life are. (And as brotherhood and ordained priesthood are, too, for that matter.) I can live a life of service without a life of sisterhood. The question arises again: how—in which vocation—can I best love and serve?

This journey, with its stirrings, is directed by God. God always initiates: we respond. But we have to figure out what God is trying to say. That is tough. One of the many ways God makes the Self of God or God's will known is through our feelings. That can be very tricky and open to self-deception. Getting others' views, advice, and counsel is a good idea.

I firmly believe God wants us to be truly happy and we can only be such by serving God and God's people. If I do not think I would be happy as a wife and mother or as a religious sister, I doubt God would want me to do it. The feelings of trepidation when I thought of joining religious life are part of my journey, elements leading me to look at the single life as a vocational choice.

So, how do you live the single life? How do you know if it is right, if it fits? You do not have to change the outward appearance of your life: the change is interior. Live life conscious of being a single person, single by choice. I choose to be here: is this where I want to be?

Conscious of my vocational state, I went about my business. I found people commenting to me on how happy I seemed. It made an impact on them: I hope it enhanced their day. Granted, my happy state and their remarks could be a confluence of many items—lessened freeway traffic that morning, the success of a task, a Notre Dame football victory. But it could also be God acting like God usually seems to do, through ordinary events and people. Could this be God's way of telling me the single life suits me? Maybe.

Of course the journey is not all wonderfully smooth and easy. Uneasiness arises within me. As with the other vocations, there is the fear: "What if this is a mistake? This is my *life* we're dealing with." Yes, there is no way to know for sure. It requires faith and trust in God. It can be hard to live with that, but if you're perceiving a call from God, it is worth risking your life.

I realize the single life is not one of security. There is no husband answering my "I do" and no religious community affirming my call to join them. It can be lonely. There is no one and no group that promises to care for me. I have to find out where I belong. It is risky and requires lots of trust in the workings of God. It is utter dependence on God, working without a net. But knowing God is with me, will I risk my life for God?

That brings up another area, that of community. It is one I am struggling with now. Woman and man are social beings. A wife has her husband, a husband his wife. Members of religious community have their companion members. Diocesan priests have their brother priests and their parishioners or service community. Who does the single person have? Parish family? Co-workers? Classmates? Friends? Members of one's birth family? Is that all? Is that enough? That does seem to be quite a number of people. And you can be very close to them.

It can also be a challenge to live celibately and chastely. With all people, how do you love and show that love in a fitting way? You have to find a balance between being cold, distant, and frustrated, on the one hand, and being overly aggressive in showing your feelings on the other. As one of my friends said, "Does that mean you won't date anymore?" It depends on what dating implies. Of course I can spend individual and personal time with people—men included—but each person makes her or his own decisions about how to live out her or his life and vocation.

The single vocation also carries the responsibility of availability. Not bound to spouse, children, or religious community, you may find yourself with extra resources, especially time. You can choose how to use them. Again, a balance must be found between hoarding that time and losing that time. But realize the obligation—or rather, the opportunity—to serve as a single person.

Other people will question one's call to the single vocation. Why would a person want to be single, choose to be single? I do not know; I cannot fully explain it. Calls from God do not always come with absolute certainty and clarity. Do you not like men? Oh, I love men, especially some in particular. I get "warm, fuzzy" feelings like any other person when I am around someone I feel attracted to. However, I do not feel called to marry these men. I can see them and want them to be good, intimate friends of mine, not husbands. Intimacy is not blocked out of a person's life: it is channeled and expressed in various ways.

Trying to find discernment assistance for the single vocation also makes the journey an effort. People heading toward married life have family support (parents wanting to become grandparents), support from the future mate, and archdiocesan, diocesan, and parish personnel directing them in marriage preparation. The period of engagement gives more time and structure. People who feel drawn to religious life have archdiocesan or congregational vocation directors who will share the journey. Novitiate or seminary life gives time and structure for discernment. In both vocations, there are structured discernment time and people who have trod the path before to share their journey.

These are lacking for the single vocation. There is no partner or community, usually no archdiocesan or diocesan office given responsibility for seekers of this vocation, no accessible trailblazers who share their stories. Only now is the single vocation slowly coming into its own, being recognized as a choice and not a default, not merely a way station until you choose what (or who) you really want to be. I feel blessed to have come upon people willing to listen to me and to challenge me.

There is still some slighting. As people have told me, "A single person can always change her or his mind and get out of it. You just get married or join religious life." If one chooses, though, the single vocation can be undertaken with the intent of honoring that commitment. It is just like the other vocations: you can get out of them, too. One can be divorced and receive an annulment, leave a community, or be laicized, but that is not one's intent upon entering.

It is not easy. You have to work at it. If you make it through the interior doubts and exterior questioning and truly hear that lovely call from God, then what? I can see a public commitment, a vow ceremony. Just as a wife and husband publicly declare their love for one another in matrimony, as a priest is ordained, and as a religious vows herself or himself to a community and way of life, a single person could vow herself or himself to the single way of life. Stand up in front of the assembly, ask for their prayers, celebrate and share with them a response to God's call. (There is a rite, "Consecration to a Life of Virginity," but I did not even feel comfortable reading it. It uses exclusive language—assuming only women are consecrated as such—and has an overemphasis on virginity. I see the single vocation in broader life terms.) There is nothing to stop a person from writing her or his own vows.

As with any other vows, vows to a single life limit oneself to a given stance and are therefore risky—you are risking your life on it. Yet making those vows is a grace-filled experience. You are not doing it alone but through God's grace and with the support of the assembly.

I see it as a covenant, a one-sided, unconditional promise to the church at large. There is no specified "other"—no mate, no religious body or community—receiving these vows before God and the assembly. It is pledging with nothing guaranteed in return but with trust in God. No one agrees to take on responsibility for that person.

Again, who is the community? Who is accepting the vows in a concrete way? Who are you vowing to? *What* are you vowing to? Just no sex? It is much more positive than that, but each person must decide for herself or himself. It is not "more holy" because of all you are "giving up for God." Our God is a God of abundance, not a God of denial. God does not want martyrs; God wants happy, loving people. For me, for now, this is the way I choose to respond to God's call to live my life. It is how I feel I can best love: God, others, and myself. I feel comfortable as a single person. I do not get that same feeling when I picture my life as a wife and mother or as a religious sister. Again, maybe those feelings are telling me something, and I should listen to them.

The single vocation is risk, vulnerability, poverty. It is a recognition that God can, will—indeed, must—provide. And God will probably do most of that providing through ordinary people and circumstances—through life.

So next time you are at Eucharist and you "pray for vocations," broaden your view and remember us—the single people—on our journey to serve God and God's people.

12 Capturing Our History, Claiming Our Future

Jo Ellen Heil

> You should work at the project that will make your heart sing.
> Lady Bird Johnson, Conservationist, Former First Lady

Some of my best friends are dead. Not morbid at all when you learn I'm a historian. Since my specialty is Women's History, I count Harriet Tubman, Mary McLeod Bethune, Fanny Crosby, and Eleanor Roosevelt among my best friends. Whether soldiers, composers, scientists, or labor leaders, they're quite a bunch.

Introducing these friends to others is the endeavor that makes my heart sing. I believe their examples give us courage today and hope for the future. Knowing they overcame obstacles in their lives reassures us during our own disappointments. Their humor frees us to laugh out loud. Such an endeavor entails recognition, naming, empowerment, and going forth, a process vital for us as women, single adults, Christians.

Whether writing or lecturing, traveling or researching, I have a professional goal that remains the same: recapture our heritage before it is lost forever, share it with those who will hear. This vision began to form during my early twenties. As a Christian, I wanted to encourage others to stand upright like the bent-over woman in the Gospels. As a feminist, I yearned to break down barriers of ignorance and racism. I was sure God would do grand, successful things through my career.

Such desires have been severely tested over the years. Looking back, I see how detours and roadblocks created a wide variety of colors in my rainbow of work. Now in my late thirties, I realize how God's sovereignty and timing, vastly different than my own, helped define my aim and refine my motives.

I have yet to see my deeply held desires come true. Lighthearted jokes about my "noncareer career" are bittersweet. My dreams have been carefully hidden at times, tucked away beneath the daily routine. There were times when I wondered if they were still there at all.

Such dreams are not only career goals, for work is a vital expression of my identity. It reflects my spirit and personality. Employment provides social acceptance and validation, since I'm single by choice and don't fit into cultural ideals of couple or family.

At the same time, I struggle to realize I'm a person of worth because God loves me, period. Who I am should not be measured by what I do or whether I'm highly paid or even paid at all. When my career goes well, I need to remember it's not a sign of God's special favor or of spiritual superiority to those around me. As with all of us, this struggle for acceptance and self-concept is ongoing. I find I'm becoming more comfortable with who I am as I grow older.

Individuals from the rich tapestry of Women's History have given me strength to face my life struggles. The bravery of slave Harriet Tubman encouraged me to finish grad school. Remembering that Fanny Crosby composed thousands of hymns when women couldn't be ordained caused me to ask hard questions during church meetings. Eleanor Roosevelt's advice, "You must do the thing you think you cannot do," convinced me to travel alone cross-country. Knowing that Mother Jones led hundreds of workers to rise up against oppression gave me courage to speak up against inequity at work. Some of these efforts ended in success, and others did not, but the sense that this "great cloud of witnesses" cheered me on refreshed and consoled me during periods of isolation and discouragement.

What is Women's History? The gathering of the stories of over half of the human race, stories smothered in silence through centuries of neglect. A diverse, multicultural weaving that embodies the Navajo proverb "Women hold up half the sky."

Society's denial of our worth lures us into camping in deserts of self-doubt and depression. Women's History provides us, women and men, with streams of life-giving water. We draw from these waters to know who we are. By recapturing our past, we name our present reality and claim a "future filled with hope" (Jer. 29:11).

Knowing feminist history is so wonderful; it makes us feel less lonely and keeps us going.

Anne Wiltsher, English historian

Early on in life I saw little difference in my love for God and a passion for justice. As a child I experienced an early spiritual conversion and was inspired by my parents' activism.

During my college days, God introduced me to the joy of Women's History during a class entitled "Women in the U.S." That was all it took. Here was my own heritage, recaptured, with more players than I'd ever imagined! God and I affectionately called it "herstory." During grad school I plunged into a multitude of rich discoveries. Crossing differences of culture and time, I met scores of women whose feelings and struggles were strikingly similar to mine. Puritan Anne Bradstreet's love poems touched my heart even as I delighted in Amelia Earhart's commonsense approach to singleness. Immigrant union organizer Rose Schneidermann provided me with insight into the camaraderie of working women. Mary McLeod Bethune showed me the power of believing in God's vision of yourself. She began one of America's first black colleges by selling sweet potato pies.

I needed their examples. It wasn't easy to be taken seriously as a scholar. In spite of a supportive committee, the path was rigorous, our History Department conservative. Some professors made jokes about what an educated homemaker I'd be someday; others suggested I might want to go into banking as a teller instead.

As a new discipline, Women's History was looked on with suspicion: I was the first at college to specialize in it. One research paper, "A" work, was given a "B" because it wasn't real (white male) history. To my vindication, it later won the department's annual Herodotus Award.

Despite these and other obstacles, I vowed to finish my education. My love of herstory got stronger. I dreamed of traveling and lecturing, sharing my sisters' stories, inspiring the public, and galvanizing the church.

After graduation in 1980 with a master of arts in history, the world of work hurled itself against my dreams with insidious force. I was now "overqualified," trying to market skills no one wanted. Part-time office experience from student days forced me to advance my most marketable skill: how many w.p.m. could I type? I reluctantly entered clerical work on a full-time basis, reassuring myself that it would only be temporary. It consumed the next decade.

Ironically, my new work home was our local Schools Office. Throughout my late twenties and on into my thirties I circulated books and films, promoted vocational education and senior speakers, wrote handbooks for youth employment programs. I provided the office support that enabled others to teach, travel, network, and climb the ladder of opportunity. As a good friend said later, "You were allowed to sit on the riverbank but not wade into the water."

As time passed, I began to question myself and God. Where was that vision of herstory? Was it a mockery? I had sensed God's leading so strongly during college. Was I now doing something wrong? Or not doing enough? My favorite saying, "One lives in hope," tarnished around the edges.

But God hadn't forgotten the dreams we'd whispered about late at night.

> Don't hesitate, but in the name of everything noble go forward and you shall have our warmest sympathy.
> Rev. Antoinette Brown Blackwell,
> First Ordained Protestant Minister

The seeds of God's encouragement had actually been planted during my last year in school. While researching a paper entitled "Is God an Equal Opportunity Employer?" I was astonished to uncover resources like *Daughters of Sarah* magazine, *All We're Meant to Be*, and the Evangelical Women's Caucus (EWC). Here were committed Christians, both women and men, raising their voices for equality. Upon joining EWC's Southwest Board, I was suddenly taken seriously as a single woman, a historian, and a Christian. I was valued as a whole person. My vocation was recognized.

I blossomed. Editor friends encouraged my writing. I began traveling to occasional conferences as a workshop leader. I met professional writers and speakers, leaders in the Biblical feminist movement. Encouraged, I began networking with community groups. I became a member of the National Women's History Project and Women's Heritage Museum.

My infrequent but enthusiastic audiences grew. I received more calls from teachers, civic activists, and Bible study leaders requesting presentations. March, National Women's History Month, became a busy, happy celebration as opportunities to share both herstory and my personal faith arose. People were touched and changed.

Those persistent foremothers were right there, watching my progress and cheering me on. I laughed out loud one afternoon while reading Katharine Anthony's *Susan B. Anthony: Her Personal History and Her Era*. Elizabeth Cady Stanton's earliest advice to Susan B. Anthony before she embarked upon her first suffrage tour was to practice, get lots of exercise, sleep well, eat carefully and to dress loosely. Lucy Stone advised her to remember her earlier speeches which were always attentively listened to, to develop her power of expression so that subjects which were clear to her could be clarified for others.

Unfortunately, none of this was frequent or profitable enough to live on, but with backers like these how could anyon⌐ doubt it was work that made my heart sing?

But back at the office I couldn't ignore the tension that was accumulating. During the work week I took pride in bringing home a paycheck and being self-sufficient. Overall, my co-workers were conscientious and fun. I helped promote education, something close to my heart, and enjoyed a good reputation in a number of departments. At the same time, I learned it was wiser not to be too open or knowledgeable about my "other" career.

Logistics were difficult. I hoarded what meager vacation time I earned or simply took time off without pay to attend conferences or to present lectures. Networking calls were made during quick breaks in the back room. Professional correspondence was literally sandwiched in during my lunch hour. Research was something I fell asleep over at night. Budget cuts led to frequent layoffs and rehirings, tense times of self-examination, and economic upheaval.

Writing consumed more and more of my time outside the office. It was no longer a passing hobby but a passionate communion with the Creator. I began to take this gift more seriously: I invested in a personal computer, organized my files, and started building up a quality home library. One of my earliest workshop outlines grew rapidly into a book-length manuscript, *Women and War*.

My work life took on a schizophrenic quality. Weeks of faithful clerical puttering butted up against hope-filled moments of conference delight. Was I a library assistant hidden among the stacks, a cog in the educational machine? Or was I the applauded professional, questioned by her appreciative audience?

Where was God's timing in all of this? Over and over doors of opportunity seemed to open up, only to allow me a glimpse inside and then to slam shut. I was nothing if not stubborn. I remained obedient to the vision. Surely it would come to pass soon.

A phone call in 1987 invaded my life. I was to be the recipient of the County Commission for Women's annual Alice Paul Award. I would be recognized as the educator who had most promoted Women's History throughout our county. After stammering my thanks and hanging up, I sat in stunned disbelief. Recognition. An award. Not the Nobel Prize, to be sure, but it couldn't have been any sweeter. I escaped to the women's restroom and laughed through tears of joy. I told God it would look great on my resume.

Public recognition galvanized my spirit. I wanted answers to the conflicts I lived with and worked around. If my vision of sharing herstory was indeed a vocation, I wanted direction and clarity. If it was something I'd made up myself, I wanted those desires taken away so I could move on with life.

Determined to seek the very face of God, I decided to attend a local one-day retreat. No one would know me or why I was there.

Since the theme was Jesus and Women, I figured it had to be for me. When I heard that the regular speaker had canceled, I wasn't so sure. I became even more skeptical when her replacement announced she'd changed the focus. We were to specifically discuss the Samaritan woman at the well. I decided to stay: I was already there and my spirit was hungry.

She began. "Jesus knows the desires in your heart. . . . Jesus accepts you, a single woman, and meets you where you are. . . . As an outcast you are the first person to be given, and proclaim, the Good News of His Messiahship." Point after point, she was the vehicle God used to anoint my day of seeking. I was overwhelmed with a sense of God's presence and involvement in my heart's desires. By the end of the day this I knew—God was intimately involved with my dreams.

During prayer at the close of the retreat, I realized afresh that herstory was indeed my vocation. That was a comfort. But like the Samaritan woman, I knew God was calling me to take bigger risks than I'd ever attempted before. That was scary.

> You must do the thing you think you cannot do.
> Eleanor Roosevelt, Humanitarian, Delegate to the United Nations.

I left my job with the Schools Office. On June 1, 1988, I embarked on a 2 1/2-month, self-financed research trip across the United States. Four months in the planning, my itinerary allowed me to wholeheartedly pursue women's contributions to America's wars.

As I crossed the California state line and drove on into the desert in pursuit of my warring women, I let out a whoop of joy. I had no idea who I would discover, but I knew they were out there waiting for me. I had no clue as to how my economic future would be provided for, but I'd never felt so free in my entire life.

Driving alone, I visited twenty-one states and dozens of sites and spent more money at copiers than I cared to remember. I stood at the edge of the Grand Canyon; I wiped away the spray from Niagara Falls. There were more warriors out there than I'd dreamed of. Spies, nurses, laundrywomen, and sailors introduced themselves through museum displays, in hidden corners in library basements, and even on highway signs. Park rangers, secretaries, and cemetery caretakers encouraged my quest. Boxes of resources began piling up on the car seats. I returned home safely after 9,343 miles.

Once home, my commitment to writing increased. I was rewarded to see my name in print in national magazines. I discussed possible movie and television scripts with an interested agency. (Very exciting though ultimately unsuccessful!) I thought seriously in terms of other book-length projects.

Then came 1989. Taking risks because of herstory gave me courage to face my most tumultuous year. God left no area of my life untouched. The pastor of our small, struggling church had a nearly fatal stroke. Her absence left us without a spiritual shepherd for months. I fell in love for the first time and then said good-bye. Close friends and significant mentors died of cancer. Recurring joint pain in my hands and wrists made it difficult to write. Missionary friends returned from overseas after experiencing bitter disappointments. Single friends I'd known for years flooded me with details of their courtships, then married and ignored me completely.

Eleanor's encouragement, "You must do the thing you think you cannot do," helped me face these broad challenges as I attended funerals, chose to stay vulnerable, made hospital visits, and attempted to be faithful in the circumstances placed before me. God used that advice to help me mature and encourage me to persevere in hard tasks.

Once again, my deepest risk taking took place in the area of work. After returning home, I'd accepted a part-time job back in the Schools Office. It gave me a small income and time to write. I shared faith discussions with interested co-workers. An innocent-looking memo changed all that.

At first reading, I didn't understand it. After it was explained, I understood too well. Our Media Library divided itself into two sections, the front being where two female co-workers and I handled a wide host of duties that helped keep the library going. The back section housed the inspection equipment. Our delivery drivers, all male, worked there. The memo stated that the drivers would receive upgrades. That meant pay raises although their jobs hadn't changed. Our front classifications were to remain the same, despite the fact that our work load had radically changed with the arrival of computers. My co-workers told me they'd not had a classification upgrade in four years. The drivers had received annual upgrades.

There was a second discovery. Despite the fact that our positions required far more expertise, versatility, and public contact, the men's jobs were already classified at higher pay ranges. Perhaps this was simply a mistake that could soon be rectified, I thought. I inquired about an appeal or the availability of a grievance procedure. With the support of our immediate supervisor, my female co-workers and I pursued appeals for job upgrades. My sense of justice was aroused. I hadn't driven across the country alone or survived 1989 for nothing! Wouldn't this be a great opportunity for God to work?

The appeal process was a grueling test that stretched over fifteen months. Female workers in other departments complained. Male workers felt threatened. Hopes were alternately raised, only to be dashed as the hierarchy continued on, slow and all-powerful. In the end I was the only one left battling. My final appeal was denied.

God had brought me to yet another place of risk taking. I was obedient and, according to the world's standards, had failed dismally. I realized in a new, albeit painful, way that who I was wasn't confined to work. In 1991 the Schools Office laid me off for the last time. Wasn't God's timing still best? God's will still sovereign?

It was finally beginning to sink in. I was a person of worth because God loved me, whether I was compensated justly, published, publicly recognized, or not. With that understanding came freedom. It was time to move on again. There were lots of new things for my hands to do.

I shall not grow conservative with age.
Elizabeth Cady Stanton, Suffragist

God continued to be in the business of expanding my vision through the Christian justice community. I became a member of Christians for Biblical Equality (CBE) and presented herstory during international conferences. Through CBE I was invited to lecture at Aston University in Birmingham, England, the thrill of a lifetime for any Anglophile. I worshiped alongside singles activists and authors and was deeply affirmed as a single adult.

That visit spurred me on to complete my second manuscript, *When Hymns Were Hers*. An inspirational workshop subject from the start, *Hymns* recaptured the stories of an international host of hymn writers, poets, composers, and translators who happened to be women. "Just As I Am," "Jesus Loves Me, This I Know," "Have Thine Own Way, Lord," "Blessed Assurance": their writers' lives had long been forgotten, yet the hymns remained famous. Singing in church became a unique affirmation. Fanny Crosby, Frances Ridley Havergal (England's "consecration poet"), and Lena Sandell were dear friends now. They'd become lively, original foremothers of faith, individual faces in the book of Hebrews's "great cloud of witnesses."

I galloped through musty hymnals searching for women's names, delighted in the fulfillment of God's vocations in their lives. I was awed at the wide impact they'd had upon their world. Here were women who'd not only contributed musically, but participated in international revivals, spearheaded literacy and Sunday school movements, introduced revolutionary theology, lived full lives despite physical disabilities. I shared their stories and was equally thrilled as these musical workshops were enthusiastically received. Someday I hope the manuscript *When Hymns Were Hers* will also be enthusiastically received.

During 1991 I decided it was time to make herstory instead of researching it. I volunteered with Habitat for Humanity, a housing ministry made famous by Rosalyn and Jimmy Carter. I became part of one of fifteen Traveling Work Camps. Alongside a work crew of three other single women, I helped construct seventeen new homes, and renovated ten others across the Pacific Northwest, Rockies, and Great Plains. Covering twelve states and led by enthusiastic retirees, we survived construction work in fifteen towns in fifteen weeks during the blistering humidity of summer.

I saw what women of hope could accomplish with their hands, sweat, tools, and hearts. The "feminization of poverty" was no longer a faceless blur of statistics. Single mothers became proud home owners with hammers in their hands. Disabled fathers stood upright in spirit as they painted. Our lives were radically changed.

Risk taking became graphically physical. I forced myself up shaky ladders, installed attic insulation, and passed buckets of wet concrete underneath houses. I persevered when work was taken out from under my hands by male workers. I ate, argued, laughed, and prayed with people of great diversity. Constant, intense media exposure forced me to develop greater poise and clarity. In preparation for it all came my next manuscript, "Tools for the Building: Meditations for Those who Build."

Risk taking: as Eleanor said, doing "the thing you think you cannot do." By whatever phrase, it was scary, exhausting, and usually misunderstood by those around me. What surprised me was the intense satisfaction, confidence, and sheer courage that welled up from deep within my spirit as I was obedient to God's promptings in these new areas. Much to my amusement, I realized that, like Elizabeth Cady Stanton, I would "not grow conservative with age."

> The successful woman remembers yesterday with pride, lives today
> with enthusiasm and looks to tomorrow with confidence.
>   Hallmark Mug, gift from a single friend

As you've probably guessed, some of my best friends are still dead. I still aim to recapture Women's History from oblivion and delight in sharing that heritage with those who would hear. I still dream of encouraging others to stand upright and struggle deeply because I remain unheard and unrecognized. I continue to be encouraged by those who have gone before.

These days I try to see myself as God sees me. Who am I as a single woman? That vision is much bigger than the boxes society would place around me, especially boxes labeled job or career. Being an adult necessitates taking risks and letting go of those very things that are held onto as most precious. Being a whole person involves believing in God-given dreams while being faithful in the daily discipline of nonrelated employment. It isn't easy, certainly not glamorous. Some of it doesn't seem to make sense at all. But it's always worth the work.

Late one night, I came across the following verse from English hymn writer Frances Ridley Havergal in Tileston's *Joy & Strength*. A single believer, she expressed sentiments that echo my own life's prayer:

> Yet take the tiny stones which I have wrought,
> Just one by one, as they were given by Thee,
> Not knowing what came next in Thy wise thought.
> Set each stone by Thy master-hand of grace;
> Form the mosaic as Thou wilt for me,
> And in Thy temple pavement give it place. (1986, 129)

Like Frances, I'm not sure how all the stones fit together, but I do know that the Great Crafter will make a brilliant mosaic of it all. I believe herstory is the most treasured jewel I can offer.

Let us recapture our heritage and use it as a building tool. With Christ as our foundation, we can use our foremothers' stories as ladders to climb over the walls that hinder our wholeness as Christians, single adults, and women. In listening to one another's stories we *can* claim the prophet's "future filled with hope" (Jer. 29:11).

13 The Single Woman in Ministry

Pamela Ann Moeller

I grew up expecting to marry and pursue a career. I also grew up in the church, singing the liturgy. By the time I reached my teenage years, however, I found the church insufferable and irrelevant. On the contrary, my love for singing led me to choose vocal music education as my profession. I taught music for one semester, when quite ironically I was offered the opportunity to "try out" theological education at New York's Union Theological Seminary. What slightly rebellious young prairie woman could resist the opportunity to spend a year in New York City, all expenses paid? I had no idea of what to expect, certainly not that the end of my trial year at Union would bring with it the inescapable conviction that I was called not to music but to theology.

That call was for me an awareness that I would not choose my vocation (indeed, I had earlier "chosen" a career in music) but was chosen for it by God. My sense of being so called, and my response, were clearly predicated on my spirituality. Specifically, both were grounded in my Union experience of finding, for the first time in my life, that I was loved by God and neighbor and belonged to the community simply because I was present in it. Recognizing this gift of profound connection with God and creation moved me into my decision to answer the call and to pursue ministry.

"Ministry" is a multivalent term. It is in the first place service to God and God's people. Such service can include both ordained and lay functions—for instance, pastoral, administrative, teaching, or even music ministries. Ministry can also be the performing of one's "secular" career in congruence with one's theological framework. As well, a particular ministry can be full or part time, paid or volunteer. Although I wasn't certain what particular shape or shapes my ministry might take over time, recognition of my call included acknowledging that my ministry would be a full-time career of doing theology as an ecclesially validated vocation.

By the end of my second year of theological study, my commitment to ministry felt quite solid. Even as I fell in love and planned marriage, I remained clearheaded enough to name as fact that my primary reality was shaped by my call to ministry and that I understood the marriage to be an expression of the ministry. I anticipated interweaving career and relationship to the mutual enhancement of both aspects of my/our life and knew that playing down my career for the sake of the marriage was not a viable option. Any apparent need to do that would indicate problems in the relationship rather than with the career.

There were times when the weaving worked. But often the threads tangled and the pressure to subordinate my career to the relationship was strong. Over time, I found myself being erased—my self as committed to ministry, my self as spiritual being, my self as woman. I rejected that erasure, and it is perhaps not surprising that dissolution of the marriage came as my career took a new tack and I moved into doctorate studies in preparation for teaching in a graduate school of theology. I spent the next five years reorienting my career from pastoral ministry to academe while finding my way out from under the trauma of dissolved partnership and into authentic singlehood.

I may be too new at the mix of singlehood and career to be certain about all its aspects and dynamics. I am certain of my self-definition, call, and commitment to ministry, which are inseparable from and indefinable apart from my spirituality. Personally and professionally I am a woman of faith, experiencing myself as beloved of God and committed to living in loving, dialogical relationship with God and therefore with others. I am as well a theological woman, a woman theologian, focusing my life work on experience of, reflection on, and action congruent with this fundamental relationship between God and humanity.

This interconnectedness is for me both boon and bane. It is boon because there is no false separation between my spiritual self and my career self, no compartmentalizing, which leads to a disintegration of self. What I personally experience, feel, believe, think is largely integrated in content and process with what I do professionally. Experience in the academic institution where I studied theology led me to my career commitment. My faith nurtures me in my career, sustaining it and challenging me ever anew toward greater professional authenticity and accomplishment for the sake of others. I do this career *because* I believe what I preach, *because* I am moved by the passion of my spirituality. That is not to say that every thread of my spirituality is content for the classroom. Moreover, I also teach outside of and beyond what I believe. Nevertheless, my spirituality underwrites my teaching in the first place, focuses me in my particular disciplines of liturgy (including such elements as prayer, praise, baptism, and communion) and homiletics (preaching). My spirituality frees me to teach a variety of perspectives and empowers my passionate and prophetic call for radical inclusivity as fundamental to the claim of Christian gospel.

At the same time, my professional work nurtures my spiritual being. It was, after all, commitment to my career that refused to allow my identity to be erased by the perceptions, interests, and needs of a singular other or of society. In carrying out my ministry, I consistently find new ideas and encounter new experiences that feed my spirit, enable me to abandon or reconfigure old beliefs that no longer serve to create or sustain health, and empower me toward renewed commitment when I encounter obstacles. Working in a field in which theological inquiry and research are expected, answers—at least in significant part—my quest for integrity predicated upon a coherent theological matrix out of which to live my life. Teaching people how to create worship events that give life rather than death addresses—at least in part—my personal conviction that "good" worship events are fundamental to healthy human being. My anguish over sexism and other oppressive injustices finds a remedy—at least in part—in doing feminist theology, which I define (borrowing some of the thoughts Eleanor Haney expresses in *Vision and Struggle: Meditations on Feminist Spirituality and Politics*) as theology that is prowomen, aims to abolish all oppression of and injustice toward persons, groups, and our ecosystem, and works toward wholeness built on love. In short, my search for wholeness as a single person and in authentic relationship with others and environment is nurtured by my professional life, even as my professional life is moved and sustained by my spirituality.

This mutuality and interconnectedness of spirituality and career can also be a bane. For women in ministries such as mine, this downside is evidenced by the fact that the church can be a hostile environment for us. Much of the church has found it difficult to welcome women as preachers, presiders, administrators, and theologians in the first place. Moreover, the more women function in these roles, the more women are naming church structures and processes, liturgical patterns and texts, pedagogies, confessional statements, and definitions of God and human relationship as bound to male being, thinking, and doing. They are seen at best as lopsided perspectives and manifestations of spirituality and relationship with God, one another, and the world, at worst as lies deadly to the whole cosmos. Out of experiences of erasure and struggle for self-definition, women discover that scripture repudiates the idea that God can continue to be defined only or predominantly by male terminology. Some also find insistence upon the definitive incarnation of God in the male Jesus an intolerable claim, as it precludes women participating in divinity. The age-old absoluteness of the classic trinitarian formula "God the Father, God the Son, God the Holy Spirit" as the bottom line for Christianity suffers heavy critique, efforts at revision, and even outright rejection. Additionally, like women everywhere, women in theology increasingly challenge the church's definitions of personhood and relationality. Many are no longer willing to accept marriage, let alone male-dominant marriage, as the norm for relationality. Recognizing that women have for too long submitted to the authority of others, many Christian women reject hierarchical descriptions and constructs requiring obedience. As Sallie McFague proposes in her book *Metaphorical Theology: Models of God in Religious Language*, some of these women choose a definition of God as Friend. They then commit themselves to building relationships, structures, and processes that evolve out of equality and mutuality, as Mary E. Hunt describes in her volume *Fierce Tenderness: A Feminist Theology of Friendship*.

Unfortunately, women who critique patriarchal theology and practice often become targets for the hostility of those who are deeply invested in androcentric constructs—men and women alike. Many find their careers are on the line, and constantly need to weigh what they must say and do at the behest of their spiritual integrity against the need to survive professionally in order to continue working toward systemic change and growth. Along with career, spirituality is also jeopardized. One's convictions and behaviors are battered by the denial and repudiation of both novices and professionals in the field. One's sense of identity is assaulted by continued use of traditional, androcentric theological language, expectations, behavior patterns, ecclesial structures, and liturgical formulas. Even women who try to carry on a "traditional" ministry without taking on the role of prophet (who names reality anew) often find the resistance, lack of support, and absence of nurture to be overwhelming. We are all likely to be painted with the same brush and named as radical (read non-Christian) feminists (read men-haters), even though we represent enormous diversity of experience, opinion, and belief. The result of such categorizing is that gospel, church, and one's own spirituality—meant to be sources of life, strength, and wholeness—all too often become sources of great anguish.

Academic institutions that train persons for ministry are by nature a hotbed for spiritual struggle and growth—all the more so with the advent of women students and finally, in most such institutions, women faculty. As the sole woman professor at one theological school, I regularly heard women's stories, was confronted with women's pain, suffered harassment, and was challenged to explain and justify women's claims and to validate my own authenticity as a "doctor of the church." Alas, I do not have answers to all the questions of theology that are now being raised, both inside and outside of the classroom, by the spirituality of women. I do function daily in the realm of deep meaning and explosive affective dynamics, walk a thin line between fluid metaphor and absolute definition, and live my life in a matrix that frequently seems half mine field, half garden of priceless treasures, often without knowing at any moment which half I'm in.

I am tempted to do either of two things: to abandon my career for one in which spirituality and profession could be more easily distinguished and kept separate, or to let the desire to survive in the career stifle the spirituality—to put all but "safe" spirituality under lock and key, therein avoiding some of the risk of confrontation and targeting. But for me neither of these is an option because I believe, finally, in what the gospel proclaims: that in Christ I experience the love of God for humankind as the ground of being, as absolutely inclusive and as calling for embodiment in structures, processes, and relationships that generate equality and fullness of life for all. I came into my career and I stay in it because I am committed to this gospel and its embodiment, because the Christian community brings me closer than anything else to this reality and provides a locus for me to study and live it in ways that cannot be reproduced elsewhere, and because I must and can aid in the transformation of patriarchy to loving justice in church and society.

Yet significant issues remain for me, issues common, I suspect, to single career women all over. How does one establish and retain balance within the dyad of spirituality and career? How does one find and keep balance in the relationship between career and personal life? How does one create and sustain friendship and solidarity sufficient to keep one nurtured and whole?

The first issue, of healthy balance between spirituality and career, has much to do with one's locus on the theological (or spiritual) continuum in comparison with that of the ethos in which one works. The more congruent the placements are, of course, the easier it will be to retain balance. However, when one's spirituality calls into question some significant aspect of one's career or, conversely, when the ethos of the vocation—such as the theological academy, church, or tradition—resists or denies the validity of a fundamental aspect of one's faith, one can find oneself caught up in a real tangle. When spirituality interweaves with career, any critique is both a professional issue and an intensely personal affair. The work of keeping self-identification, energies, and perspectives strong in the face of frequent assault on that which shapes one's being—all without succumbing to ideology—is a strenuous exercise. So also is the effort to stay honest with one's passions while maintaining the necessary distance that keeps the self from being fractured with every blow experienced in the workplace. Walking the fine line of integrity without either underwriting patriarchy or sabotaging oneself requires inordinate skill. Where do we find the requisite training?

The second issue is also a matter of balance—that between the work of one's career and the rest of one's life. Ministry (though hardly unique in this regard) is never done. Everywhere there are urgent, even desperate, needs to be met. People are dying out there for want of gospel, I tell my students, and who would contribute to their deaths? So I do everything I can to equip my students to bring life. That means long hours in the classroom, in meetings, in one-to-one conversations with students around academic issues and personal problems. Students must be able to think theologically, but helping them sort through the legion and often subtle perversions of gospel is not easy. One must read extensively and publish as well. Moreover, faculty in theological academe are expected to serve the wider church. Because women in many ecclesially validated ministries are still few in number, many get showered with "invitations" from every congregation, committee, or agency that needs a woman member or resource person. Additionally, when people we meet on vacation, in grocery stores, and in libraries discover what we do, they manifest the curiosity and interest that signal opportunities for ministry—particularly regarding the inclusivity of gospel. The result is that especially for women, the demands are often nonstop and overwhelming.

With both these issues, the stakes seem higher for a single woman. The lure to commit all one's time and energy in order to survive (let alone flourish) beckons almost irresistibly. Additionally, others often assume that a single person is available to do what someone with partner or family wouldn't have time to do. After all, no one else clamors for my attention, no one else makes demands upon my time, no one else calls me to accountability. And it *is* far easier to fail to create time for rest and re-creation and/or to renege on one's commitment to oneself for some time away than it is to disappoint an intimate, especially when the balance of spirituality and career is regularly in jeopardy. Moreover, going home to an empty house at the end of the day can make it far harder to shut down the spirituality/career software of heart and mind than going home to a partner does. How effortless it is to fall again into the trap as women have so often done: in the face of others' need, to give until one erases oneself!

The third issue arises from the first two. Support mechanisms, and especially friendships, are essential for single career women, but they are also difficult to create and to sustain. Women in ministry are often isolated as the only woman on the faculty or the only woman pastor in town. If we are not one of a kind, in many places we are still a small minority. It is difficult to find persons who share enough of our experiences and views to help test out ideas or correct excesses of perspective or zeal. Members of our particular constituencies provide real support and sometimes real friendship, as do women in parallel positions elsewhere, but there are many times and places in which they cannot stand in solidarity with us. Often they, too, are struggling for survival and simply cannot take on anyone else's issues. Those acquaintances that do occur require a great deal of already scarce time and energy to develop into true friendships. Moreover, mobility is a particular hazard for single people. Rarely do relationships move with us, and sustaining them at long distance and in dramatically different contexts requires extraordinary commitment. We struggle to build and sustain networks, but often our resources are too limited to put or keep relationships in place. Thus much of the time we are left to struggle on alone or with only fragmented support.

On the personal scene, the single individual who lives alone is always the bottom line. Particularly in a society that still centers itself in marriage and nuclear family as the paradigm for relationship, single women, especially clergywomen, find it hard to meet people outside of career involvements and to develop relationships that might provide greater balance to life. People don't know what to make of us, are sometimes intimidated by us, or perhaps think we are so self- or God-sufficient that we don't need friends. Yet the hunger for human touch and tender loving care can become overwhelming and, if unmet, stultifying of both person and career. Teddy bears and plants help make a house hospitable and warm, but they are not good at massaging the knots out of one's neck or providing affirmation or healing for a soul exhausted or fractured in the struggle. Nor can they provide basic economic support if one's spiritual integrity leads to professional disenfranchisement. Certainly nothing guarantees that any of these supports will be there in a partnership. Yet having experienced some of this succor in relationship (despite the flaws and faults), as a single person I feel the absoluteness of the nonexistence of such sustenance.

How much more freely might I work if the supports were there? How much more energy and creativity might be available to me apart from and in my career if the balance were more readily sustained? Much work yet needs to be done to free women like me for full experience of wholeness.

But there are benefits of the single career woman's reality. Being single can make career decisions relatively easy. One is not biased or limited by relational commitments to stay or go. Others are less likely to become victims of whatever costs one pays in order to pursue one's work. Nor are efforts to dismantle patriarchy compromised by primary relationship with those still largely invested in androcentrism. Few distractions annoy or drain away limited time and energy. I enjoy considerable freedom to schedule my time. My daily, early morning hour of race walking is never co-opted by another's needs: my vacation time is of my own design and never compromised by another's expectations. I enjoy the luxury of focusing on the career and spiritual self in tandem—I do what matters most to me, and what matters most to me finds expression in my work. While one is sometimes compromised for the other, neither is ever seriously neglected. My career provides me with a primary source of spiritual nurture. The gospel claim for wholeness is content for my career as well as address to myself and so supplies both reason and courage to say no when I need time for myself. Commitment to women and to authentic singlehood strengthens my resolve to survive, and not just to survive, but to flourish. The knowledge that I have integrity and self-definition apart from a singular other and androcentric societal norms empowers me and others to new confidence.

I believe the realities of single women have helped and continue to help make possible significant movement toward the wholeness of persons, church, and society. The struggle is by no means over and our gains may be precarious. Yet women's stories are more valued than ever before, as are the claims, theological and otherwise, that come from women's experience. Women are finding ways into more and more kinds and levels of career. Women have greater respect for one another, honor our diversity more, are increasingly able to be accountable to one another and provide support for one another. Single women are finding it easier to build and sustain friendships with men and women, singles, partners, even whole families. In spite of the obstacles, we continue working toward deepening spirituality, revising old and creating new names, ideas, structures, and processes that embody mutuality rather than relentless confrontation. Our efforts work similar change in the church, in the world. We begin to see ourselves as interdependent and mutually accountable not only to one another but to the global community and to the entire ecosystem. Progress is not fast, and there is enormous work to do—but it is happening. The more women stand in solidarity with one another toward justice for all, the more hope we have of accomplishing that aim.

V Loneliness and the Rewards of Solitude

In a society that promulgates instant stimuli and thrives on constant togetherness, solitude is an anomaly, is suspect, and is to be avoided at all costs. Single women can witness not only to the value of solitude in their own lives but to the deeper meaning solitude provides for the growth of the spirit so lacking in modern times.

In "From Loneliness to Solitude: Reflections on Aloneness," Gwyneth Griffith analyzes the differences between loneliness and solitude and presents solitude as an opportunity for experiencing our rootedness with other women, the earth, and spiritual reality.

Since her divorce, Mary O'Brien has realized that solitude is at the heart of her single life. It is solitude that gives richness, meaning, and balance to her life, enabling her both to celebrate herself and to serve others. Mary offers a fresh perspective on intimacy.

After a lifetime of loneliness, Lila Line finds solitude by making a best friend of herself. Lila recounts the success of her six-year journey.

14 From Loneliness to Solitude: Reflections on Aloneness

Gwyneth Griffith

In Volume III of *A Woman's Notebook*, I found a quote by Ellen Burstyn: "What a lovely surprise to discover how unlonely being alone can be" (1983, n.p.). I discovered that quotation one recent summer morning as I sat on the screened veranda at my cottage overlooking the still lake and hearing only the sound of the birds, an occasional fish jumping, and in the far distance, trucks speeding down a highway. I was writing in my journal, cherishing another day of being alone, and reflecting on my life and my feelings. As I near the age of sixty, having lived alone for most of the past decade, I have come to value the quiet, reflective times.

I began writing in my first journal ten years ago, as I withdrew from my regular life for several weeks to complete work on a thesis.

June 19/81   6:45 A.M. At "my" spot at the end of the point. A crow woke me at 6:15. I surprised a huge heron standing on the rocks. A big fish just swam by, reflecting the mood of the morning—calm lake, no sign of sun on it, a soft warm breeze—the crows reminding me that all is not calm and beautiful. A beetle floated by two minutes ago, legs moving so not yet dead, and the fish just caught it for breakfast. I'm finding it hard even to kill ants these days. I have a sense of wonder about all of God's creatures and how we all interrelate. This is such a precious time. I don't want to go back to the city today even temporarily. I'm not sure what feeling closer to God means, but I do know I feel filled, at peace, both content to sit and ready to get going on the day.

Yet just two days later after my visit to the city:

June 21/81   Aloneness has not felt as fulfilling since yesterday when I came back up from [visiting a close friend, who "loaned" me her dog to keep me company]—that deep wrenching feeling of loneliness which causes not just tears, but sobs, "I'm so lonely." It's good to have the dog with me although I feel the loss of the absolute freedom of the aloneness that I had. I have to let him out, make sure he gets exercise, isn't too lonely etc. etc., yet the affection of another living creature—and it's mutual—is a comfort and a joy. I find the cloud and stillness a comfort and I seem to need comfort today.

And again two days later:

June 23/81   After all the rain, the closed in-ness and the depression I woke to clear sky, sun, wind and clear fresh air, and I feel fresh and whole, my "self" again.

The experience of aloneness can be a positive or negative one depending on a number of factors. As was my experience in the journal entries shown, a single woman can move quickly from feeling good about being alone to feeling devastated and back again, sometimes there can be a mixture of both feelings, or we can have a basic stance toward aloneness that affects our whole way of being and attitude to other persons and the world.

North American society, on the whole, does not value being alone, except possibly for the eccentric genius or mystic. Single women are still often pitied because we do not "have anyone to be with." Dictionaries often reflect the prevailing mores of a society. Funk and Wagnall's *Dictionary*, for example, in its 1956 edition, did not distinguish between loneliness and solitude. Although "alone" was defined simply as "without company, solitary," "lone" was defined as "standing by itself, unaccompanied, solitary. Single, unmarried; usually of women, with humorous or pathetic implication, as in 'poor lone woman.' " "Lonely" meant "sequestered, solitary, dreary, desolate. Solitary or addicted to solitude, sad from lack of sympathy or friendship." The assumption remains in many quarters that everyone would be with others if there were a choice, especially in relation to a partner and family. And many single women are still isolated, seen as a threat to the married, as witches were in the Middle Ages.

As I began work on the theory base of my doctoral thesis, an exploration of relationships with particular relevance to education and power, I discovered a changing perception on the part of some. Clark Moustakas, in his 1961 study, defined loneliness as an experience of being human that enables the individual to sustain, extend and deepen one's humanity. He stated that "loneliness is within life itself, and that all creations in some way spring from solitude, meditation and isolation" (x). He acknowledged that there was loneliness anxiety and that fears of loneliness are fed by a way of life that centers on acquisition and control. He felt that being lonely in the positive sense requires "a total submersion of self" (8). As I reread this study thirty years later, I realized how much he was reflecting on male experience, especially his own. By 1972, when he wrote *Loneliness and Love*, he distinguished between two aspects of existential loneliness. He referred to

"loneliness of solitude" which is a peaceful state of being alone with the ultimate mystery of life—people, nature, the universe—the harmony of wholeness of existence, and "loneliness of a broken life," suddenly shattered by betrayal, death, pain, separation, death and crisis that severely alter not only one's sense of self, but the world in which one lives, one's relationships and work projects. (20)

Moustakas also recognized the dangers in the kind of analysis he was doing:

The truly solitary process is not tangible and materialistic; it cannot be defined and quantified. It remains aesthetic and mystical. The moment it is studied and "understood" it becomes something else, something radically unlike the original solitude, with all its vague/diffuse visions and dreams, with all its imaginings and wondering and its incomprehensible powers that sensitize and cleanse. (1972, 41)

As I reflected further, I also realized that it is through journals and poetry that the reality of aloneness and community, loneliness and solitude is most sharply portrayed. It was in the late seventies that I was introduced to the journals of May Sarton. I found especially in *Journal of a Solitude* that the richness of her experience as a single woman and her reflections on her life called out from me a new awareness and possibility. I had always struggled with a deep fear of being alone, of being left, partly of not having someone to "take care of me" and of not having any identity except in relation to other persons. Sarton did not hide from the realities of loneliness in her aloneness, but she also deeply valued her solitude:

I am here alone for the first time in weeks, to take up my "real" life again at last. That is what is strange—that friends, even passionate love, are not my real life unless there is time alone in which to explore and to discover what is happening or has happened. Without the interruptions, nourishing and maddening, this life would become arid. Yet I taste it fully only when I am alone here and "the house and I resume old conversations." . . . This is what frightens me most when I am first alone again. I feel inadequate. I have made an open place, a place for meditation. What if I cannot find myself inside it? . . . My need to be alone is balanced against my fear of what will happen when suddenly I enter the huge empty silence if I cannot find support there. (11–12)

My own reflection on interdependence explored the positive and negative aspects of dependence and independence and how they may be combined in ways that are both valuable and harmful to persons. The writing of a doctoral dissertation is a very solitary activity, and my own experience was interwoven into the writing. I became aware that solitude is essential for life in community. In the dissertation, I wrote:

In interdependence each of us is an integrated self with a core within which one is totally alone. The self is no longer defined by others, but it develops in interaction with others and in solitary reflection. It is essential that persons have the opportunity to communicate with and trust their deepest selves. The rhythm of being alone and together, solitary and "with" is within the context of the interdependent vision of justice, the context of action within community. One can experience interdependence with animals and the earth, and within oneself, being creative as one "listens" to both sides of one's brain and to one's spirit. There *is* no such thing as independence in the world. (319)

LONELINESS

When one is lonely, one often experiences pain, fear, anxiety, depression, restlessness, and a lack of self-esteem. When I first began living alone (not by choice), there were days when I was overcome with such feelings. From my journal:

September 2/83 Last week got progressively worse, not quite nervous at being alone but the reality sinking in. I'm either staying late at the office to work or plopped down in front of the TV drinking something. . . . I would like to do more reading as I listen to music, but I need to stop feeling sorry for myself before I can do that.

And May Sarton wrote:

Loneliness is with me. It was awful coming back to the empty house, where so much needs doing. . . . [T]he air around me feels dead. I cannot animate my life these days. I feel marooned here. . . . I feel stupid and cross this evening. It occurs to me that boredom and panic are the two devils the solitary must combat. When I lay down this afternoon, I could not rest and finally got up because I was in a sweat of panic, panic for no definable reason. . . . I am bored with my life here at present. There is not enough nourishment in it. . . . I feel old, dull and useless. (94–95)

Later she described her feeling as "being sucked into the quicksand that isolation sometimes creates, a sense of drowning, of being literally *engulfed*." (1973, 107)

Sarton noticed that the most tragic solitude for her occurred when her consciousness became a stranger to her true self and when her distress became so great that she could not say what she desired or what she lacked. For me, loneliness is a result of lack of choice in being alone and occurs when one's self-identity is dependent on the presence and responses of other persons. Those who are inclined to function in this dependent mode often see others as having both power and responsibility over them and do not have the inner strength or confidence in themselves to discern and act on what they need or want in their lives. Anne Wilson Schaef, in *Escape from Intimacy*, analyses this in the extreme in her description of "relationship addicts":

They are absolutely terrified to be alone, and when no one else is around, they believe they are alone. They therefore must move from one relationship immediately to another. . . . They find themselves spending so much time trying to maintain the relationship that they do not have the time for any spiritual life or personal growth. . . . Persons suffering from this addiction look to the relationship to tell them who they are. (6–7)

Single women who feel lonely much of the time may be caught in societal mores, believing that "two is better" and wishing that their lives were basically different from the one they are experiencing. They may be unable to befriend themselves. Jeremy Seabrook, in *Loneliness*, shares the story of one such woman, at age sixty:

I'm one of those people who aren't quite what they seem to be. I'm busy, active, I have friends. I help my neighbours, but I'm quite empty inside. I'm really a shell, there's no feeling left. I'm a withered woman, you see. I mean it, quite literally, I'm wasted. I ought to have been married. I should have borne children. It's what I wanted above anything else. And I knew all the time that my life was passing, that I wasn't fulfilling myself. But I didn't really know why, and at that time I certainly couldn't have done anything about it. (27)

SOLITUDE

The feeling of solitude is very different from the feeling of loneliness. Its value may be appreciated more when one has experienced the pain of loneliness. Its feelings are contentment, joy, groundedness in one's self and one's spirituality. Through solitude, one is able to give birth to oneself, able to offer that self to others. It is a gift, but one needs to be intentional about creating opportunities to experience it.

I am well aware of the class privilege I enjoy which has provided me with the time and space required for solitude. Economic security brings not only the privilege of traveling to special places but the opportunity to acquire books and music, to contact friends, to have vacation time. Solitude may be a special gift to the single and especially to the professional or business woman.

My appreciation and experience of solitude has developed over the past ten years and has now led to a significantly different way of life. As may happen with others, circumstances provided the opportunity and challenge to spend time alone. My story in earlier years had been one of feeling isolated within groups, seldom really at home with where I found myself, not really feeling connected, looking to others to meet my needs. In 1981, I experienced a long recuperation from surgery and then solitary time at our family cottage to work on my dissertation. I analyzed myself as dependent, wanting to be interdependent with others but fearful of the independence that needs to interact with dependence to enable that to be possible. I would never have thought of living alone or taking a trip alone. Two years later, my housemate of long standing moved away and I felt desperately lonely. I began to take motor trips alone and discovered that I not only could function on my own but could enjoy it!

July 5/84　A difference this year is that I am more into myself, more inner directed, not as externally focused. I feel so much better in and about myself. I know I can *do* more, I am more assertive, I like to be by myself. There are ups and downs, of course. I now know the difference between loneliness and aloneness. Though lonely at times, I like my aloneness. I know now that no other person can make me feel complete. I have to feel that within myself and then reach out to others. I am finally building up my independent mode!

The deep appreciation of solitude, however, came in 1989 with a six-month sabbatical. I traveled alone in Britain for two months and spent four months in various settings nearer to home, usually alone. I read, journaled, walked, and reflected on my life as a single woman alone. Two years later, I left my position as principal of a theological school to become a free-lance consultant. I now not only live alone but work alone much of the time. Time and space alone, therefore, are necessary for solitude. May Sarton reflected on her privilege:

It is an age where more and more human beings are caught up in lives where fewer and fewer inward decisions can be made, where fewer and fewer real choices exist. The fact that a middle-aged single woman, without any vestige of family life, lives in this house in a silent village and is responsible only to her own soul means something. . . . I have time to think. That is the great, the greatest luxury. I have time to be. (1973, 40)

Our attitudes toward time and work need to change for solitude to be an integral part of our lives. Sarton echoes my own experience:

I am still pursued by a neurosis about work inherited from my father. A day where one has not pushed oneself to the limit seems a damaged damaging day, a sinful day. Not so! The most valuable thing we can do for the psyche, occasionally, is to let it rest, wander, live in the changing light of a room, not try to be or do anything whatever. (1973, 89)

My journey toward solitude involved other components. As well as time, it helps to have a special place or places to which one can go, separate from the daily routine. For me, this has been a cottage, a friend's country home, and conference and retreat centers. It could be a special spot in one's house or apartment. This provides the opportunity for a focus on the interior life and, for this, silence is an important quality. Silence, at least from the artificial sounds in our world, enables us to listen to the sounds of the earth. It is not coincidental that the large number of "Solitudes" tapes available today include the songs of birds, the sound of water and wind. Annie Dillard spent a year alone in order to write *Pilgrim at Tinker Creek* (1974). Feeling grounded in oneself means being connected with the earth. At other times, listening to music, journaling, and reading poetry and other women's journals connects us to the depths of our own spirits.

For many single women, an animal, real or toy, or flowers keeps us company. May Sarton had her dog and cats and bowls of daffodils. In her poem "Wilderness Lots" in *The Silence Now* she wrote of her cat: "She was the wildness in me, the secret solitary place where grows the healing herbs" (1988: 33). *The Little Prince* (Saint-Exupéry) found his solitary life more worthwhile through the time spent on a rose. I talk with my violets and my stuffed bear! Being solitary, however, does not mean being unconnected. Maria Harris, who has been helpful to me in reflecting further on the links between solitude and spirituality, says in *Dance of the Spirit* that women's spirituality must include connections. She speaks of

a solitary spiralling down into a deep well. But when we touch bottom, the experience turns out to be that the waters of life and spirit underneath each of our own wells are common waters where all that has divided us begins to merge. In the merging, we discover the impulse toward community. (41)

Adrienne Rich, in her poem "Culture and Anarchy," connects "my solitude of self" with "my dream of a common language" (1981, 15). I discovered that my valuing of solitude accompanied my growing appreciation of women's community. As I began to affirm myself as a woman, I experienced a sense of connectedness with all that was around me, other women, the earth, and a spiritual reality. Knowing I was rooted in community, I could rejoice in aloneness. Women are relational beings. This does not mean that other persons must be present at all times, but rather that our response to the world is in terms of being connected with it.

That sense of rootedness is essential to solitude. As well as community, it may involve feeling rooted in a place or a people. The sense of having space to go deep inside oneself is enriched by the sense of connectedness back through time. During my sabbatical, I sought out ancient sites of standing stones in the lands from which my people came. One early morning I stood alone among the Callanish stones on the Isle of Lewis in Scotland. The mist swirled around the stones and I felt surrounded by the lives of people connected to me through the millennia. I felt awe and wonder and gratitude. The experience would not have been as powerful if I had not been alone.

MOVING FROM LONELINESS TO SOLITUDE

Even if one has the privilege of finding time and space in which to experience solitude, one needs a change within. Because loneliness is related to a lack of self-esteem, the strengthening of one's sense of self is essential. Solitude is feeling comfortable about being with oneself, and so befriending that self is necessary. This requires at least one trusting relationship and support from others. From this can come an ability to risk and to be open to the unexpected, finding, in that, moments of grace.

For aloneness to be experienced as valuable, there needs to be, at least for most women, a mix of solitude and community. As we need to have a sense of ourselves in order to feel enriched by and contribute to community, we need mutual relationships with others to experience a sense of our own humanity and to lead a full life. Sarton quotes Louis Lavelle:

We sense that there can be no true communion between human beings until they have in fact become beings: for to be able to give oneself, one must have taken possession of oneself in that painful solitude outside of which nothing belongs to us and we have nothing to give. . . . Nevertheless this solitude into which we have just come and which gives us such a strong sense of inner responsibility, and at the same time of the impossibility of being self-sufficient, is experienced as a solitude only because it is at the same time an appeal toward solitudes like our own with whom we feel the need to be in communion. (1973, 103)

The move from loneliness to solitude requires diversity in the ways in which we approach each day, including both order and spontaneity. Key to the development of discipline are the recognition of personal responsibility for the way one lives one's life and the commitment to caring for oneself as well as for others. The development of one's own special rituals is an important part of getting in touch with one's deepest self. This may be easier to develop when one is away from a daily routine of work, but the challenge is to claim time for oneself within that routine. Rituals can assist us in getting in touch with the rhythms of life and the integration of our bodies and spirits.

The reality of our being body/spirits and that relationship to loneliness/solitude was demonstrated for me during the year that I went on sabbatical. One evening prior to leaving, in the midst of hundreds of people, I suddenly became immobilized as I pictured myself alone in a strange city. I was terrified in the anticipation of extreme loneliness. The feeling did not pass until inadvertently I began to move around. Two months later, when I did experience strong feelings of fear and loneliness, I recalled the previous experience and intentionally went for a walk and focused on taking photographs. Although the loneliness did not all disappear immediately, I felt able to cope and after writing some letters to friends, was able to continue my solitary journey with joy and contentment. As I felt coordinated in my body, as if everything was moving together, I felt good about myself and my spirit became more whole.

Because solitude is intimately connected with our affirming of ourselves as body/spirits, as whole selves in relation, it is a crucial component of spirituality. For me, the affirmation of my times of aloneness was accompanied by my openness to intuition, to waiting for the movement of the Spirit in my life, to spending time reflecting on the deepest issues of life. We who have been doers, who have needed to control everything in our own lives and often those of others, find it difficult and frightening to wait, to "wait upon God," and to be patient, open to surprises, the serendipitous. In my nurturing alone time, I discovered strength and joy in my inner depths, an openness to and appreciation of creation, and the presence and power of the Spirit.

Maria Harris quotes May Sarton: "Loneliness is the poverty of self; solitude is the richness of self" (1989, 183). A single woman, especially one who lives alone, may experience both in her aloneness. Loneliness is inevitable at times. Solitude is a gift that can come with choice, self-esteem, acceptance of personal responsibility, the nurturing of community, and often with class privilege. Not only loneliness can come with the ending of an intimate relationship but also the strength that results from the acceptance of aloneness and affirmation of solitude. It is important to acknowledge the painful feelings of loneliness when they sweep over us. But as women connected with one another in our deepest selves, we find strength in our times of being alone. This enables us to offer selves that are more whole to the community.

15 On Solitude and Other Things

Mary O'Brien

I was a latecomer to the single life. Following a divorce after sixteen years of marriage, the whole direction of my life changed as I began to explore how to live as an "uncoupled" person and to search for meaning in my new existence. Living alone, without partner, without those routines and justifications which are so much a part of marriage, was a whole new experience. I had perceived much of my early adult life, before marriage, as an interlude, "waiting" for the right person to come. Cultivating my own individuality, exploring my needs, seriously developing and pursuing a career had been subordinated to living in expectation—hardly a preparation for singlehood. Hence, much of my energy following divorce was absorbed in the search for a new identity as a single person.

This process involved a great deal of reflection and experimentation, often quite painful while at the same time challenging and full of expectation of the unknown. The women I befriended who had carved out creative lives for themselves after divorce became my mentors and models. These were the people who enabled me to realize that despite the risks involved in the single life, I could rejoice in the autonomy it provided.

Then a challenging career opportunity presented itself that involved taking another significant risk. I chose to take it, and four years after my divorce, I moved from the United States to Prince Edward Island in Canada. My two children, who were well on their way to adulthood, chose to stay in the States, so for the first time in my entire life, I was living alone. It was here, in the peace and quiet of this beautiful and pastoral little island, surrounded by ocean in the far reaches of Canada, that I could ask myself the questions that had been waiting for the right time and circumstances to be raised. I not only began to confront "What am I going to do with the rest of my life," but the more important "*How* am I going to live the rest of my life? What am I going to include in my everyday existence and what will inform my decisions as to what that existence will consist of?" These were not entirely new questions. However, my previous life had been largely dictated by demands placed on me by family, working toward a degree, and trying to establish a career. Although I had made some important choices in the past, I now had the opportunity to structure, plan, and organize my life more consciously, with more deliberation as to its meaning and purpose. I felt I also had the responsibility and the obligation to ask myself what kind of a life-style would enable me to grow as a single person and, at the same time, to give the best of who I am to others, to friendships, to my career, to myself.

This tiny island was, in many ways, the ideal place to reflect on these concerns, and over the next few years I pursued a spiritual journey that for me was unique. All of my life, I have sought that which is of the spirit, a meaning to life, a relationship with God, and how I could best work out that meaning and relationship in my own daily life. However, this experience was of a different kind from any before. What would give meaning to my *single* life? What would enable me to live on my own and be satisfied and happy? So, for the next two years, I began to discover what has become, for me, the essence of the single life.

While I was in the process of making the decision to go to Prince Edward Island, a friend asked me why I wanted to go there. Without any hesitation or conscious reflection, I replied, "For the solitude." I was somewhat surprised at my response, but this did become the focus of my new journey: to seek solitude. Perhaps the most important thing that the island experience taught me is that solitude is at the heart of my single life. I learned that this is what gives richness to my life and provides its meaning. Certainly solitude was nourished by the very nature of this tiny island—the quiet, the ocean, living close to the land and to nature, the remarkably strong and creative people I came to know who were also nurtured to a great extent by this same solitude. Solitude became my friend from which my life seemed to flow. It informed the rest of my life by pointing a way for me to balance my inner life and that which is directed outward. It became not just a segment, but an integral part of my life—like eating, working, playing, and praying. I began to realize that solitude allowed for reflection, preparedness, appreciation, awe, and reverence. It enabled me to develop an awareness, an alertness, an attentiveness to life, a new way of seeing and listening. And at its best times, it brought a harmony, a unity, and a oneness that I had never experienced in such totality.

Of great importance to me was the coming to terms with self—befriending myself in my aloneness. In one of her many journal-memoirs, *Recovering: A Journal*, May Sarton reminds her readers of the significance of solitude for achieving self-identity, for establishing a good and positive relationship with one's self. I have found this to be one of the loveliest discoveries: in solitude, I can and often do enjoy my own company, my own friendship. I have also discovered that solitude brings forth and affirms for me my own uniqueness—who I am, where I am going and why.

I would not be honest if I said that solitude is all joy, that it is once and for all attained, and that it is easily sustained. Solitude involves a commitment that has to be affirmed again and again. There are times when I do not feel capable of being faithful, for even though solitude can inspire elation, it can also induce anguish. It is a two-edged sword with its own demands, often gratifying and rewarding, but sometimes overwhelming and seemingly harsh.

Paradoxically, it is in solitude that we become more deeply and keenly aware of our common humanity. Since moving in and out of solitude can give a renewed strength and depth and sensitivity to relationships with others, it is also here that I often feel the sharpness of the pain and suffering of other human beings, whether it be that of a friend or a victim of war. It is also in the silence of solitude that I confront my projections, my losses, my unfulfilled desires; here I am forced to let go and just let life be. In solitude I have also to learn to confront my own aloneness, to accept the life I left behind and the one I have chosen, with the sometimes terrible realization that life is really where I "pitch my tent" in the wilderness, not necessarily in isolation, but alone. When I choose solitude (and I do believe that, in order for solitude to be meaningful, it must be chosen), I have to say "yes" to my aloneness. However, my island experience began to teach me the difference between loneliness and being alone and to allow loneliness into my life as a friend and, sometimes, as an adversary. When I welcome loneliness as a friend, I find that it can teach me patience—the patience of waiting, of being willing to plunge into that part of myself that speaks without words and to reach for that which is often unattainable. This kind of loneliness can enrich solitude and can add to its meaning. It can lead to understanding of and, I hope, a greater compassion for what my life is about. It also brings me closer to a great truth of life: that each one of us is essentially alone and that each of us has to find her or his own way in that aloneness. However, a loneliness that paralyzes and is crippling is another matter. It seemingly has no purpose. Perhaps it is a sign that there are other things in my life with which I must deal and that, for the moment, solitude is not a healthy place for me to be.

Solitude and being alone are not necessarily one and the same, nor is solitude merely a result of living alone. I think solitude is an invitation given to every human being that has less to do with geographical place and space and more to do with an inner attitude and stance toward self and the world. Hence, solitude is a choice. It is a choice to affirm my aloneness, my singularity, to allow the silence of the moment to speak its own special message. Even though every person has a need for solitude, my singlehood allows me unique opportunities to make this choice and to weave solitude into the fabric of my everyday life. Occasionally it means saying no to others. It also means that I try not to use other people and things as distractions to satisfy my restless nature, to fill in the aloneness or the boredom that can be part of any life with its disciplines and routines.

Solitude, though, if it is not to be taken to extremes, must find its own balance. It is not an end in itself, nor is it meant to be an escape from life in the pursuit of my own individuality and perfection. It can be a way of discovery of self, of others, of one's relationships to all of creation, and ultimately of God. "In solitude," says Meinrad Craighead in *Weavers of Wisdom: Women Mystics of the Twentieth Century*, "our deepest intuitions of an indwelling personal God Spirit are confirmed, the Mothergod who never withdraws from us and whose presence is our existence and the life of all that is" (16). I find that it is in the silence of that solitude that all things can become sacred. However, unlike the great mystics, artists, and writers whose creative output demands a very solitary life, the rhythm of my life is determined by my work, which is not entirely solitary, by my response to other necessities of my life, and by my need and desire for friendship. One thing I learned early on is that in order to live in solitude, I must also have community and, as a single person, I have to take the responsibility for creating this community. So, solitude has its own rhythm, and if I listen to those rhythms with honesty and attentiveness, I learn when to move out and when to come back.

Each person who chooses to include any measure of solitude in her experience needs to explore that which enables this solitude to become a creative part of life, that which sustains and supports its growth. I have come to realize that amidst all the changes and upheavals I have experienced in the last several years, prayer has always been the thread that winds through my life, giving groundedness and continuity to my reality. If solitude has become the heart of my single life, it is also a preparation for prayer, for one flows into the other; each gives the other nourishment and meaning. Because I live alone in a life that includes solitude, prayer has taken on new and different meanings for me. It has become less dependent on words and more dependent on being present to the Other, present within and without.

Although I believe in the importance of the practice of prayer at fixed and specified times each day, I have also come to realize that my whole day, my whole life, can be prayer. Prayer is not an action performed at one time of the day, it can *be* my day. Prayer can be the way I relate to others, the way I prepare a meal, the way I take care of my home, the way I listen to the news, read a novel, listen to a piece of music, contemplate nature, or gaze at a work of art. Living prayerfully means listening, hearing, seeing with a certain intensity, awareness, liveliness. It also means being able to take what is being heard, seen, and experienced into my very being and to live and suffer with these things. For me, this intensity flows from the daily practice of prayer, from taking the time each day to listen in a special way to that silence within myself and the quiet around me, alone and in solitude. I have found that if I am faithful to prayer I am more in touch with the Source of my being; I have a greater clarity as to who I am and what I am about. Without the habit of prayer, I become alienated from my own creative source and that which brings me into oneness with others and all of creation as well as my Creator.

A great help in nurturing solitude and prayer in my life is a retreat where I go every year. I spend one or two weeks at a monastery deep in the woods of Nova Scotia, renewing my spirit through reading, reflection, prayer, and being close to nature. It is a special time for me to follow the psalmist's bidding, "Be still and know that I am God" (Psalm 46:10).

Prayer puts me in mind of ritual, those acts whereby each of us celebrates certain events in our daily lives by according the event a particular meaning, often through enacting a distinctive ceremony and celebration. People who live in community with others have built-in rituals around eating together, celebrating important occasions together, and praying together. Sometimes these are planned and sometimes they are spontaneous. As a single person, living alone, I have a strong need to create ritual, to ritualize certain ordinary events and, at times, the important occasions of my life. Some of the rituals I try to initiate are around prayer, by creating my own ceremonies. The artist Meinrad Craighead finds nature a source of her spirituality and thus her art. She has an altar in her garden, and each day at dawn, she lights a candle and then watches the sun rise. Feast days are of particular importance for her to ritualize, and she does this by enacting her own ceremonies. I too try to enact rituals around those feast days that are important to me, in particular, Christmas and Easter, the two feasts that provide a very special rhythm and meaning to the cycle of the Church year and to my life. I find books such as *Woman Prayer, Woman*

Song by Miriam Therese Winter and *Women-Church* by Rosemary Ruether helpful in performing ritual around prayer. Music can also become part of ritual. Important to ritual is the clearing of a special space, for rituals are, each in their own way, distinctive and sacred. They require some thought and preparation.

Rituals also provide ways for me to take care of myself, for being good to myself, at times treating myself as special, as I would a guest in my own home. I think this kind of caring is essential to the single life. I make a ritual of meals, especially dinner. I feel that although the food one is eating (or serving) is important, almost more so is how it is served. So when time permits, I try to create a warm ambience with candles, music, and sometimes flowers. The very act of lighting candles can be ceremonial. In *Gratefulness, the Heart of Prayer*, David Steindl-Rast speaks of the ritual of lighting a candle while one is alone as of particular significance, a prayer which can be appreciated to its fullest only when one is alone. The point is that our ordinary lives give opportunity for us to celebrate through ritual those occasions that are meaningful to each one of us.

I mentioned before that essential to my solitude is the realization that I also have community. As a single person, my immediate community is not knit together by family ties, so I strive to develop friendships with a variety of people from an equal variety of backgrounds. This effort, which is so necessary to my well-being, takes time and energy. I need to share with others who I am, and I need to let others into my life to share with me who they are. My friends allow me to give and to receive, to be part of their lives, to laugh, at times to cry, to rejoice, and at times to share another person's misfortune. I find special kinship in the friendship of other single women like myself who understand, often in unspoken ways, the joys and struggles of leading a single life. However, for the past several years I have been part of a discussion group made up of persons who are searching for a deeper meaning to the spiritual life. As the only single person in this group, I have grown to appreciate the friendship of the married couples. Their shared experiences of life are often heartening and encouraging, and their married life-style is often juxtaposed to my single state in such a way that we can learn from one another.

Discussing friends brings me to a subject that I know is of concern to most people, but in particular to those persons who, like myself, live alone. It is the subject of intimacy and how to achieve it as a single person. When we discuss intimacy in our culture, we often do so in the context of persons and usually in the framework of sexual intimacy. I think that most single persons (and probably many married persons) would agree that there is no such thing as real sexual intimacy outside of a committed relationship with another human being. However, I have discovered, and am still discovering, that intimacy does not necessarily have to involve other people.

I think that the psychoanalyst Anthony Storr, in his book *Solitude*, is on to something very important when he points out that the assumption in our culture that it is only through intimate interpersonal relationships that we can find fulfillment often prevents us from finding intimacy in other significant areas of our lives. Although most of the examples Storr uses to validate his hypothesis are of great men who were writers, composers, or artists, much of what he says does strike a strong chord in me as a woman.

My work provides real intimacy for me. I recognize that I am fortunate in that my work helps me channel my creative impulses and allows me to put life and reality into many of my ideas. I believe that the potential for this kind of intimacy is available to both women and men, whether single or married.

I have found that there are many other sources of intimacy open to me in my everyday life if I take the time (and have the energy) to create them. I am a person who lives very much with and through my senses. My home and how it looks and feels, the sounds I hear and all that surrounds me are very special sources of intimacy. I have spent time making my surroundings look pleasing to my eye and be a comfortable place for me to live. I have lots of plants that give me joy and that I consider my friends. All of these things are truly sources of intimacy for me. I agree with Sheila Cassidy's insights in *Sharing the Darkness* that what we surround ourselves with is a reflection of who we are. My home is a nurturing place and space for me, and I enjoy sharing it with others. It is a way of sharing with them another part of myself, a way of saying, "This is also who I am."

Another source of intimacy for me is books. I always have read a great deal of both fiction and nonfiction. My single life has made me a more avid reader and particularly of literature by women. Music also creates another source of intimacy, delight and nurturing of the spirit in my life, particularly since I have been single. Yet another great source of intimacy that has grown in importance to my solitude and spiritual life is nature. I live close to a lake and a very short distance from woods. Long walks, sitting at the edge of the lake, and watching the morning mist rise are just a few of the activities that have become part of my life. My relationship with nature is not just a backdrop to my life; it has become a significant and essential part of my life. Through this relationship I have become more aware of the interdependence of all living things, plant and animal, rock and mineral. I have come to feel a need to protect this life as it nourishes and endows mine with its beauty and its vulnerability and speaks to me of a living God.

However, the greatest asset or gift I have found in the single life has to do with choice. I can come and go when I choose, and I can choose when to be alone and when to be with others. I can also choose who I want to be with, what music to listen to, how to arrange my habitat as well as the rest of my life, for that matter. These choices are possible because my life is not directly circumscribed by the needs of others. Choices, though, stand the risk of becoming selfish. It is easy to live my life just for me, and often I do. However, since becoming single again, I have tried to think about, pray about, and reflect on what my responsibilities as a single person are to myself, to others, to the broader community. I have come to some realization of what I need in my life, given my temperament, to enable the spirit to grow within and without and to meet my God in my life. However, I continually have to ask myself what enhances and what diminishes a praxis of concern and caring for others and then try to find ways of making and activating certain choices. Is my life really focused outward and not just inward on my own concerns and needs? Am I allowing who I am to enable others? Am I too self-involved and living too much for myself? These are not questions asked once and for all. They create the dialectic and tension in my single life and they are ongoing. They are the ones that require an honesty and a willingness to act upon that honesty, and even then I am never sure.

Singlehood is an invitation and opportunity for each of us to seek and risk the unknown within ourselves in a world that often questions the validity of the single life, especially for women. It demands a commitment to care for oneself and to go beyond: to care for and about others as well. The single life does not promise ease or comfort or certainty but has its own rewards: offering each of us the opportunity to develop unique and creative life-styles that attest to and affirm who we truly are. To live a fruitful single life demands discipline, just as any other kind of life does. It means living alone while creating community, a seeking of balances amidst ambiguity. Singlehood asks us to seek intimacy in far-away places and in our own homes. At the same time, it allows for growth in clarity, in single-mindedness. It is a confirmation of the reality that solitude and aloneness are not only a part of life but are necessary and enriching. Thus, when lived intentionally, the single life can be a unique witness—one that I believe is very much needed in today's world—despite all its paradoxes.

16 Solitude: A Most Welcome Gift

Lila Line

My visit to New Hampshire was the first trip I'd taken when I began living alone after my twenty-eight-year marriage had ended and two of my three sons had married. My youngest son was attending college in New Hampshire, the reason for my visit.

Thelma Babbitt's name appeared in *Directory for Traveling Friends*, a publication of the Friends General Conference for the purpose of accommodating Quakers from all over the world. She lived in a one-story redwood house that dated to the early 1800s. The long, narrow house meandered along a hillside at the edge of a mountain. Beside one end of the house, firewood was stacked eight to ten feet high and covered by a wide lean-to roof.

Thelma greeted my traveling companion, Mary, and me with a gracious and inviting smile. I was struck by the youthful appearance of this tall, slim woman with thick, grey wavy hair. Inside the house, a small wood stove warmed the kitchen and two nearby bedrooms that were furnished in antique oak and bright blue and green quilts. The rest of the house was closed off to conserve heat.

While eating a light supper in her large country kitchen, Thelma disclosed that she had lived there alone since she had become widowed some thirty years before. She was now seventy-five. As Mary told of her work as a professional artist, Thelma listened intently, her hands folded in her lap. Somehow, I sensed a great deal of serenity in this woman. After I told her the reason for my visit, that I had recently begun a career in writing and, most of all, that I was also living alone and feeling painfully lonely, I asked, "Don't you ever get lonely living here by yourself, Thelma?"

She shook her head and smiled. "Why, no indeed!" Her blue eyes sparkled. "Why, I've got these mountains," she waved a hand toward the windows, "and the trees and birds and a beautiful lake nearby to go canoeing on, and so many good friends. No," she repeated, "no, I never get lonely."

I returned home wanting what Thelma Babbitt had. Although I'd felt lonely most of my life, I was now feeling more alone than ever before. Granted, I did not feel lonely when I was raising children, attending college while the boys were in school and working at part-time jobs, but once my sons left home, I experienced long periods of intense loneliness and occasional bouts of depression.

My husband and I had never learned to communicate. At that time, there were few books about marriage and communication and the marriage counselors were of no help. Further, my husband met few of my needs. Soon after the children left home, we were divorced. I never liked city life. When I became single again, I moved from my home in Washington, D.C., to a village along the shores of the Chesapeake Bay. When I had discovered Maryland's Eastern Shore a short time earlier, I fell in love with the farm lands surrounded by miles and miles of waterways. I didn't know anyone living in the area when I rented a small waterfront cottage. There were times when I was so lonely, I could not bear to sleep there. I'd call a friend and drive back over the Chesapeake Bay Bridge to spend the night in familiar surroundings. Eventually, I met people and was able to remain in my own home but still I felt deeply lonely much of the time.

For a long time, whenever I complained about my loneliness to Mary, she would simply say, "Thelma Babbitt." Although I heard her message, I wasn't yet prepared to grasp it. I continued desperately to try to alleviate my loneliness through other people. So that I would not be alone during the day, I taught writing classes in the adult education department of a nearby college. Evenings, I worked in the registration office. My students and the other employees became my family. But when Friday night rolled around, the unbearable distress plagued me like a chronic illness.

A divorced friend confided that she dealt with the problem by setting up activities for the weekend in advance. Somehow, I didn't plan ahead, hoping that someone would call or drop by or perhaps that that knight in shining armor would suddenly appear. When that failed, a tightness in my throat, a knot in my stomach and a feeling of panic engulfed me. In a frenzy, I'd finger through my address book and dial numbers.

After a long while, perhaps because I knew that the serenity I so desperately craved was attainable or maybe because I'd suffered long enough, I took the first steps. I sought counseling. I also read a number of books that were helpful and joined a Quaker Friends Meeting that has given me a real feeling of belonging.

Later, I would complete a twelve-step program for adult children of alcoholics and dysfunctional families (ACOA), and more recently a program for people who are codependent (CODA). I was led to the program when a family member, addicted to drugs, went into treatment. By attending meetings, going to conferences, and talking with people with similar problems and after much prayer and meditation, these dreadful, lonely, empty feelings began to dissipate.

But my recovery did not happen all at once. Along with the support of friends and people in the groups, I found others with whom to share both the good and bad times. I met Dianne at a party a publisher had for contributing writers. Although Dianne lives sixty-five miles away, we meet often for dinner. She joined others to celebrate my having won a five-thousand-dollar prize for a nonfiction book, *Waterwomen*, depicting what life is like for five women who work the waters of the Chesapeake Bay for a living. At the party was Mary, with whom I have spent dozens of afternoons, watching as she painted, supporting one another through one crisis after another. Also at the party was Sandy, a former student who a few months earlier had spent the night with me at a motel in a strange place. At four the next morning, we climbed into a motor boat and went out on the Chesapeake Bay with a woman who netted fish, the first of the women profiled in my book. Then there was Phyllis, a highly gifted young widow with dark hair and large brown eyes. She refers to me as her mentor because I encouraged her to continue her studies through graduate school. Her second book is about to be published.

To celebrate my prize, my friends joined me in a dimly lit upstairs room of a local pub, ordered wine, set a bouquet of flowers on the table and toasted my good fortune. We bit into thick, juicy hamburgers garnished with tomato and globs of mayonnaise and treated ourselves to a dessert of large slices of cherry-topped cheese cake. In a poem written the next day, Phyllis captured the event. She wrote:

Lila: She sits across the table.
There are others; but mostly it is Lila
flush with success.
First prize for her book! In that dark Jewish brilliance
I catch glimpses of
my old friend Ann,
my only friend through high school.
Lila's words fall as a dressing

on old wounds,
familiarly
like strokes of an old
tom cat who closes his eyes
remembering the feel of
his mother's tongue.
I am telling things
never told to old friends
and laughing so loudly
I must cover my mouth
while her eyes burn
like nuggets of anthracite.

Unfortunately, even with the taste of success still sweet upon my lips, I began to wake again each morning with a grey cloud over my eyes. I remember returning home from a trip to New England one August after leading a workshop at a conference. While saying good-bye to one of the women there, I moaned, "I dread going home alone." The woman, in her late seventies, admonished, "Why, you're not going home alone, Lila. You're going home *with* you." I would later learn that she was right.

Now I can look back to the place where my painful feelings began. The third and youngest in a family deluged with both emotional and physical illness, I felt that my mother resented my birth. When I was in my teens, she confirmed my suspicions, telling me she was never able to love me. Looking at baby pictures, I wonder how unlovable I could have been. I have come to realize that it was not me that she could not love as much as her circumstances. With my father chronically ill and my sister often sick with a childhood disease and complications, she was unable to pay much attention to me. Through counseling, I am working to forgive her. She did the best she could. Yet the neglect has left its mark. I strongly believe that not getting my needs met in childhood is responsible for my deep loneliness. John Bradshaw, a noted counselor in the field of dysfunctional families and recovery, points out in his book *Homecoming* that if our inner vulnerable child was hurt or abandoned, shamed or neglected, that child's pain, grief, and anger live on within us.

Besides feeling neglected, I felt a great deal of shame. Initially, that shame resulted from my family nicknaming me "Monkey." They claimed I was born with hair all over my body. The hair disappeared, but the nickname remained. I remember my father holding me up to a glassed cage in a zoo when I was about five. I recall telling them, "I don't look like that." They laughed. To add to my problem, while I was told I was unattractive, even ugly, because of a large nose, straight black hair, and thin legs, my sister, eighteen months older than I, was admired for her small nose, wavy blonde hair, and round, chubby build. That, along with similar behaviors, left scars and a low self-image that has lasted long after the practices ended.

Because of such abuse, I stuffed my angry feelings and detached from my family. I isolated myself in a closet in the bedroom I shared with my sister. There I wrote poetry to my family, my way of trying to bond with them. Now when I speak to schoolchildren, I tell about being a "closet writer."

For years, I did not know that the unbearable sadness was in part the pain of loneliness. Mistakenly, I thought that if I left my parents, I would recover. A month before my nineteenth birthday, I left my family. I traveled by steamboat to Norfolk, Virginia, where I took a bus to Virginia Beach. Because we had spent summers there, I imagined I would not be lonely. I was wrong.

In order not to be alone, I had relationships with men who would be socially unacceptable to my parents, partly because they were blue collar workers but mostly because they were not Jewish. I worked as a secretary at an army post and lived in civilian barracks. Although my cold, barren room was not nearly as cozy as my room at home, it was far better living there than experiencing the verbal and physical abuse I received from my mother, who continued to slap me across the face up to the day before I left. I remained at the beach for three years. I returned home in order to end a relationship when the man I had been seeing threatened to kill me if I left him.

Though I thought of myself as a free spirit, I still wanted to please my mother. When my sister introduced me to a young Jewish man, I married him though I felt no attraction. I've always questioned that decision. I recall that when I declined his proposal, confessing that I didn't love him, my mother advised me that I was making a mistake. "After all," she said, "you're twenty-two. If you don't marry him, you may never get married."

When my future husband insisted he loved me enough for both of us, I accepted his offer. Having craved affection all of my life, it was easy to fall into that trap. I soon learned his hypothesis was incorrect.

The reason I did not voice an objection to the marriage was because I thought that if I married, I would never be lonely again. I also theorized that if I married a Jewish man, my mother would love me. I was wrong on both counts.

I knew on my honeymoon that my marriage was a mistake. Yet I remained with my husband for twenty-eight years, until my children were grown. One of the reasons I stayed with him was because I was ashamed to admit my failure to my parents. Another was my fear of being unable to support my children and myself. But my greatest fear was that of being alone.

In retrospect, I know I was alone all my married life. Though my husband was unable to meet my emotional needs, I provided a good deal of support to him, evidenced, I feel, by the fact that until we were married, he had a severe problem with stuttering. Within two years, the stuttering stopped completely. With my encouragement, he opened a ladies' fashion shop, something he had wanted to do for a long time but had lacked the confidence to try.

Finally, when my oldest and middle sons got married and my youngest entered college, I left my husband. I was led to the small village of Royal Oak in the Chesapeake Bay country. I love the water. My house is on a farm surrounded by a creek. Canada geese, swans, ducks—bufflehead, mallard, mergansers—winter on the creek, which overlooks tall pines on the opposite shore. Each morning, I marvel at the activity on the creek and am grateful that my house overlooks such a serene scene rather than a highway or city street.

Though at times I have felt that I might want to share this paradise with a mate, I am convinced that that is not necessary for my well-being. It is also a relief to know that I no longer need to search for that knight in shining armor. I remember the men who were a part of my life, from the first boy I was infatuated with at age fourteen, to dozens of others over the past fifty years. Aside from a boy I went with from the time I was fifteen until he left for overseas during World War II when I was seventeen, I don't believe I have ever felt true intimacy with a man. For a long time, I regretted not having a man in my life to share affection, companionship, and sex. Admittedly, everything is better shared. To be perfectly honest, I can't say I don't regret not having found the perfect or near-perfect mate. I only know that I can now usually replace "regret" with "acceptance." Previously, whenever I attended a social function, I'd hope there would be a man there for me. I no longer think, "Maybe *he* will be there." *He* may not be there, but I will be. I believe many women feel this way, but as I have grown stronger in self, the hope of finding a mate has diminished.

As for sex, I began having sexual dreams when I was nine or ten. Instinct taught me to masturbate at that time. I've never experienced an orgasm with a man as intense as in my dreams. I don't blame men for this phenomenon or myself. I fault society in general, my mother in particular, and the custom of instilling in children, particularly girls, that sex is bad.

Not having an intimate relationship with a man doesn't mean I don't have male friends. Bruce, a young schoolteacher, accompanies me to the movies regularly. Tom, a professional writer, visits with me on rainy days. We sit beside my wood stove and talk for hours. And at my summer retreat in the Blue Ridge Mountains, Bill calls or comes by evenings to talk about poetry and short stories or to go for long, moonlit walks.

Over the years, I have encountered women who remain in abusive relationships because of the financial security or the fear of living alone. A close friend whose husband is retired claims she never has time to herself. As much as she loves her husband, she often goes outdoors to get away from his repetitious chatter, but he follows her there. A widow acquaintance told me she dreamed her husband, whom she mourned for two years, had returned. She woke up screaming, "But I'm free now, free. Don't you understand? I'm free!" She said the dream surprised her. Although their marriage had been comparatively good, she said she realizes she is happier now than she's been in her entire life.

I am happier, too. I do what I love to do. I write and teach. My career began when I moved to the country. My first writing endeavor brought me the prize. I was fifty-seven. Since then, over a hundred of my articles have appeared in leading magazines and newspapers, and my first children's book was published two years ago. A young adult novel is presently with a publisher. My profile has appeared in a Maryland Women's History Month journal for the past six years, a real ego builder for one who had previously suffered greatly from low self-esteem.

In retrospect, I was unwittingly preparing for my career when I enrolled in a creative writing class at the University of Maryland when my third son was two weeks old. I was thirty-six. Within a few months, I went to work part-time in a government agency that paid for my education. My salary afforded a live-in housekeeper. I attended college at night for the next sixteen years, taking one or two courses a semester, all that I could handle while raising a family and working.

Education gave me the knowledge I craved. It also helped me develop a healthier self-image, important in my pursuits as a writer, teacher, and lecturer.

My schedule gives me the freedom to enjoy solitude and country living. From my lane, I peddle my bicycle three miles to the Tred Avon River, where the oldest continuously running ferryboat takes cars and passengers across the river to a nearby town. A quarter of a mile in the other direction, the Miles River stretches as far as I can see. White sails dot the horizon above boats heeled over in a brisk breeze. The deserted back roads of the sparsely populated county where I live are perfect for biking. Generally, I ride alone because I can take the time to see the trees, plants, flowers, animals, birds, geese, and bald eagles. Another person and conversation would distract me from all this. I pace my biking to my own rhythm and, finally, stop to meditate at a favorite pier.

When it's too cold or windy to bike, I swim at a YMCA at a nearby town, take yoga twice a week, and take long walks. I exercise regularly, not only because I love it but because I live alone and feel that with proper diet, that will help me stay well. When I am down with a cold or the flu or another ailment, young neighbor girls stack my wood and a friend brings me food, if need be.

I spend most of my days alone. I write from about nine in the morning until midafternoon. On my way to riding my bicycle or going to the YMCA, I stop by the post office, collect my mail and chat with the postmistress, Etta Miller. Some days she's the only person I speak to. I look forward to seeing her because she has a good sense of humor and she's as excited as I am with my acceptance letters and checks. On the other hand, a rejection slip may upset her day as much as it does mine. When I entered the contest, she dreaded the return of a manuscript. Once when there was a package that could have been a returned manuscript, she quickly told me, "Don't worry, Lila. It's from L.L. Bean."

At night, lights from a red cedar house across the creek shimmer on the water in summer and sparkle on the ice in winter. Corn grows high in the fields alongside acres of soy beans. At the shore outside my workroom window, tall reeds sway in the breeze. The tide runs swiftly during a northwest blow, and rain puckers the water's smooth surface during a storm. Swans nest at the water's edge, while a great blue heron fishes for dinner. In spring, bullfrogs croak loudly in a pond nearby and a heron sings to its offspring in an evergreen beside my window. Its low, melodious lullaby gently lulls me to sleep.

I gave up my job at the college in registration because the time spent writing has earned me far more satisfaction and remuneration and because I also wanted to spend summers in the mountains in a mobile home I bought. There I work on a novel or write short stories, a change from the nonfiction that I write for newspapers and magazines. When not writing, I move from one project to another—stacking wood, gardening, or doing other chores.

After working on my emotional health for six years, I am finally at peace with my aloneness. I acknowledge my need for friends, but I don't define myself totally by the relationships that I have or the roles that I play.

Unfortunately, in today's world, a person's well-being is almost exclusively measured by the success of her relationships with others. I measure it by the ability to live in peace with oneself.

Thelma Babbitt visited me recently on her way to a nearby country inn. When I told her how much she had influenced me, her small blue eyes twinkled and she recounted a recent trip to Europe with Elderhostel. Again, there was a sense of serenity in this vital woman so obviously at peace with her singleness.

Now, whenever a challenge presents itself, like a month-long motor tour of Nova Scotia I took with myself, I simply say Thelma's name and I'm on my way. Such was the case when I drove to Portland, Maine, to board an overnight ferryboat to Yarmouth, Nova Scotia. Once the boat got under way, I sat on the darkened deck and listened to the dozens of people talk and laugh. I felt sure I was the only person traveling alone. I gazed at the blazing stars and a sliver of a moon until my flickering eyelids refused to stay open. Then I retired to my cabin for a good night's sleep, feeling completely at peace.

Like riding my bicycle, traveling alone allows me to pace myself at what feels most comfortable to me. When I'm with anyone for any length of time without solitude, I lose my center. I feel unbalanced and slightly fragmented. At such times, I need to be alone again to savor the experience and to become centered. That does not mean I don't have friends. I do. But my well-being does not depend on my friends. It depends on me. I feel grateful that I have finally found the solitude that Thelma Babbitt described to me those many years ago. Instead of with a grey cloud, most mornings I awaken feeling lighthearted and thrilled at the dawning of a new day.

Looking back over the years that I struggled to rid myself of the wearisome feelings of loneliness to make room for the sweet gift of solitude, I recognize that it's been a long and painful journey. But I didn't travel it alone. I was *with* me every step of the way.

VI Celebrating Our Spirituality

Our spirit, or spirituality, is at the core of our existence. It is that which connects each one of us to all that is human and nonhuman. It is also the deepest expression of our uniqueness and our diversity. For single women, spirituality is expressed in a multipicity of ways.

Susan Muto outlines three steps to appreciation and understanding of singlehood. She sees the single life as a gift from God enabling us to model ourselves on Christ in prayer and service. Susan writes of the joy that results.

In "Growth in the Spirit," Tricia Ogiste traces her life from her youth in the Caribbean to her life in Canada, sharing manifestations of the Holy Spirit in her ever-deepening spiritual journey.

Vicki Morgan expected to marry and to have children. Still in her early thirties, her singleness has led her on a quest for wholeness. She writes, "Being centerd is to live out of a deep connectedness of all of life." All acts become sacred.

17 Prayer, Service, and the Single Life: A Spiritual Perspective

Susan Muto

Meeting, mating, marrying—these are the ideals many seek as ultimate, the goals matchmakers promise to make happen despite the fact that in our day one out of every three marriages is predicted to end in divorce.

In such a climate, being single, either by choice or by circumstance due to separation, divorce or widowhood, is defined in the negative. To say, "I'm single," is to say, "I'm *not* married." Yet nearly one-third of the adult population in the United States today is single.

The single life, like the married, is not a matter of indifference to what people think; neither is it a trap hampering freedom or a temptation to flee permanent commitment. From a spiritual perspective, the single life affects the way I relate to God, self, others, and the world.

That is why it upsets single persons to be treated as statistics or misfits by society and the church. An overemphasis on couple orientation and family affiliation makes it inevitable that singleness be associated with me-ism, lonely hearts' clubs, and unlimited license. Many unmarried women and men risk being labeled "losers." Because of the "marriage is best" mentality, church functions often become pious dating services rather than places to experience a good blend of social life, prayer, and service.

To live a healthy and holy single life, one needs a loving circle of friends. Social life has to complement one's spiritual life. Prayer has to be motivated and inspired by a person-to-Person relationship with Jesus Christ, who was and remained a single person in the world. Single Christians maintain their commitment to Gospel values in a world inundated by careerism, consumerism, materialism, hedonism, and secular humanism. It is hard at times to resist being pushed into lonely, unloving situations as in a singles' bar. Longing for community yet not finding it may even lead one to risk demeaning, loveless sex or to become promiscuous.

Compounding the loneliness factor in the single life is the symptom oft detected of low-grade depression. Singles must guard against its stinging influence by cultivating a sense of self-worth and a commitment to service in imitation of Christ, who came not to be served but to serve. Singleness in my experience can be seen as a gift women and men bring to the church. It heightens their capacity for respectful relationships modeled on Christ's own capacity for friendship and inclusive love.

Our faith tells us that all human beings, single and married, are singularly loved by God. We are created male and female in the divine image, form, or likeness of God (cf. Gen. 1:26–28). This means that we are formed by God and for God from the beginning. Before we are anything—priest or parent, career woman or nun, married or ever-single, widowed or divorced—we are singular human beings, uniquely created by God, called by name and longing for union with the mystery of All That Is. The awesome truth is, we are born single and we die single. No one can die our death for us.

Three steps seem to be essential starting points if singles are to renew appreciation for our own calling and promote its understanding.

First of all, we cannot look to others, we must look to ourselves to overcome prejudice and reaffirm our worth and dignity as persons. Any negative evaluation of singleness must be corrected on the spot.

Second, no person should be denied a position or function in society simply because she is single. This might mean, for instance, taking an outspoken stance against economic structures that show preference to persons who are married rather than single or being sure that single persons are included in the life of the church. It is sheer hypocrisy to preach sisterhood and brotherhood and yet to exclude single people from "all-church suppers" or from invitations to familial and cross-generational gatherings. Any single person who feels the brunt of such exclusion ought to speak up to a pastor or counselor on the church staff. Proactive singles must resist accusations that they are threats to marriages or irresponsible because they do not know what it is like to support a family. These instances of ignorance and insult ought not to be treated lightly.

Last, but not least, any flare-up of "singles bashing" needs to be confronted and overcome in ways that model Christ's vision of a loving community. Were I asked to target the core of my concern it would be this: Long after the rhetoric of rugged individualism and the "I've got to be me" of rampant narcissism have worn thin, single persons have to come to grips with who they are before God in prayer. This posture of humble listening is the prelude to any and all forms of service to church and society. Far from being devoid of possibilities, singleness can be viewed as an invitation to commit oneself to a faith-filled life open to God and others in joyful self-giving.

This blending of prayer and service is a dynamite combination. It keeps one open to the surprises of God (what I call the receptive mode) while guaranteeing that one experiences a sense of purpose (the productive mode). In other words, prayer prevents one from succumbing to the modern disease of addiction to work and achievement as ends in themselves. A sense of service enables one to rise above motivations driven by the need for power, pleasure, and possession only.

When lacking this blend of prayer and service, being single can draw one into the traps of self-centered preoccupation or sensual indulgence. The spirituality of the single life not only demands times of explicit self-examination, it also enables a person to be present to all in need of care. Being single myself, I find I have more free time to take my nieces and nephews for special treats, to phone a friend, to visit a sick person, to help others by the extra hours I spend writing and teaching. And the truth is I find more time to pray, also in the midst of my work.

Choosing to live as a single person in conformity to Christ actually promotes greater availability for ministry. It does not matter whether one is a nurse, machinist, teacher, administrator, fireman, cook, artist, dancer, or author. Not to be faithful to one's call, not to pursue excellence, would expose one to the temptation to put selfish interests and material needs above the invitation of Christ, who came not to be served but to serve.

The love singles show ought to be nonpossessive, nonmanipulative, self-giving, and compassionate, as one strives to love others with the love with which God has loved us. This means rising above the tendency not to get involved with others and truly befriending them.

While our lives may assume a definite direction, we must be open to the grace of the moment, ready to give up futile attempts to control life so that we can flow with the gifts and challenges of every new day. The single life has an open-endedness about it that plunges one at times into ambiguity and puzzlement. We may find ourselves asking in our twenties and again in our forties:

Am I really called to stay single all of my life, or is my being single merely due to a set of circumstances over which I have no control?

Am I single only because my parents need me and I must live at home?

Is the work I do not conducive to combining a career and a committed married life?

Or have I truly been called by God to be single for reasons yet to be disclosed?

These questions are part of the reality of affirming a single spirituality, though to do so is not always easy, nor are such inquiries simply answerable. Prayer helps us to take a wider view of life. It enables us to trust in a Power greater than one that sees only the next stage. When we are sustained by daily prayer, it is easier to say yes to whatever life brings, to hear and heed the inspirations of the Spirit despite the risks involved.

The worst danger of our work is that we fail or refuse to set aside time for prayer. We allow close conversations to degenerate into small talk. We swing this way or that. We depend on being "in" with the fashion of the moment instead of rooting ourselves in truths that last.

The best way of countering selfishness is for singles to focus on fostering a purposeful life of service, channeling energy to meet the needs of others while regaining stamina by taking time for prayer. This means that we must intentionally center our singleness in the heart of Jesus, the single Word spoken by the Father. In and through Christ, we are united spiritually with needy people near and far. We may be a-lone but we are also mysteriously all-one.

Far from being a negative experience of withdrawal and isolation, singleness becomes the ground of solidarity and communion. It symbolizes the single component of human togetherness. It is a pathway to realistic action and encounter. Living the single life not only makes one more receptive to God's call, it also gives one the courage to stand up for what one believes rather than allowing oneself to be swept away in the churning tides of popular opinion. Christian values will always pose painful questions to a society that mocks commitment. As a guardian of moral and spiritual values, the church, supported by single people prayerfully attuned to Christ, will be better able to resist the push and pull of a world cut off from the lived awareness of God.

Recall the lives of such single Christians as Søren Kierkegaard, Dag Hammarskjöld, Edith Stein, and Flannery O'Connor. Their singleness made them especially available to witness to Christ in philosophical, political, educational, and literary arenas. They suffered misunderstanding, but they were not afraid to stand up for what was right and to defend their faith. Such freedom carries with it a high degree of responsibility. One who lives alone must be ready to study harder, to take a few extra moments to listen to people, and to respect the dignity of everyone regardless of creed or appearance. Only thus can one become a healing presence in a broken world.

To be single in imitation of Christ is to witness to a way of living and loving that liberates us from the bondage of narcissism and allows God to use us as instruments to bring about a transformation of life and world.

Too often singleness is a cause for lamentation accompanied by long, gloomy faces and endless frustrations. One must counter such assumptions by coming to celebrate this way of life as God's special gift, opening one up to new avenues of meaning and creativity. Whether the single state is freely chosen or thrust upon one by circumstance, it offers an excellent opportunity for solitude and communion, for recollection and participation, for retreat and action.

Singleness, with the help of God's grace, can generate a joyful spirituality oriented toward effective service in church and society. It can enable us to experience moments of feeling care-free because we are cared for by God. We sense that our dependence upon divine mercy makes us more and more interdependent on one another. Our whole life becomes an act of giving thanks for the goodness of God and for the grace to stay single and faithful.

As Jesus walked along the road to Emmaus with two seekers, telling them all they needed to know (Luke 24:13–35), so we must walk with him while being willing to go out of ourselves in love for others. By sharing our burdens and sorrows, our blessings and joys, we as single persons say to our companions on the road that they are not alone, that a loving, caring God is with them always. To love in this way requires emotional and spiritual maturity and, above all, a contemplative vision of human beings as the family of God and all of us as God's children, called singly by name (Isa. 43:1).

A joyous single person is like a light on the mountain. She or he moves like a dancer in tune with the rhythms of life, its peaks and valleys. Gracious, open, receptive, gentle, joyful—with these dispositions one responds to the injunction to do the works of God and to allow God to give the increase. Some are called to serve in soup kitchens, others in research laboratories; it all depends on who we are. What matters is that we remain gently alert and quietly open to any invitation to service that the Lord issues.

We must go into the desert with Jesus, knowing all the while that the test of our relationship will come when we walk with him on the dusty road. Our meeting with the Lord in silent prayer is but the beginning of a lifelong response to being missioned. To affirm the reality of one's own single spirituality is to obey what Jesus tells us at the end of the Gospel of St. Mark: "Go out to the whole world; proclaim the Good News to all creation" (Mark 16:16).

18 Growth in the Spirit

Tricia Ogiste

As I sit here in blissful serenity, I am thankful for God's goodness to me,
and I wish everyone could be as happy. I wonder out loud, would sharing
my story help someone? I hope it would! I am sharing my story with you
today for two reasons. First, I believe when we share we not only claim
our spirituality and therefore become stronger, we help others to identify
similarities in their lives. Second, there is a Force within, greater than
ourselves, which is the God experience through our spirituality. Spirituality is a life process of coming into touch with our own unique spirit as we
live through our experiences.

Today I am living a single life and I ponder the question, Are childhood
dreams relevant to life's reality? As a child, I always admired Rose
Barriteau, who lived in a lovely little pink house surrounded by a flower
garden, mostly roses and pink anthirums. My dream was to have a house
and garden just like Rose Barriteau's; yes, Rose was a spinster. My
sister Mary wanted to be married and have children . . . just like
Mummy . . . and she did get married and has two sons. I am still waiting
for my house and flower garden; for now the plants in my apartment must
suffice.

I believe that God has a plan for our lives from conception until death.
It is an adventure to observe one's life as it unfolds at various stages and
in ways that are inexplicable. Some events in our lives we take for granted,
others we analyze to the extreme, and others we accept as inevitable and
part of the Creator's plan for us. In reflection on how my life has evolved
from childhood to this present time of maturity, I uncover some of the
mysterious ways in which God works!

CHILDHOOD

When I was about 5 1/2 years old, my father emigrated to Aruba, an island of the Netherlands Antilles north of Venezuela. Two and a half years later, my mother joined him and left her young brood in the care of her mother. My parents worked and lived in the parish of St. John's, in a village called Florida, and my grandmother lived in St. Patrick's in a little district called Marli.

My grandmother lived with her last son, who was then about eighteen or twenty, and suddenly she was a single parent to three curious children, 8, 5 1/2, and 3 years old. It was a time of adjustment for all of us, but more for us children than for Grandma. Our sheltered life of total dependence and overprotectiveness changed to one of learning to be independent. As the oldest, I had to look out for my younger brother and sister. Grandma had a farm, large enough to provide for her needs. Miss Cuddy, a dark brown cow with cream spots, was part of the thrill of this new life. She was oh, so tame and sensible that I was allowed to walk with her to the grazing pasture on my way to school and back in the evenings; that was fun! When she had a calf, things were different. As all mothers look after their young, Cuddy was no exception; therefore, walking her to pasture was difficult because Chanty (the little black-and-white calf) had to make various stops and naturally, mother followed. I was relieved of my chore, then, because Cuddy needed my uncle's strength to keep her on the path!

I attended a public Anglican school for the first 2 1/2 years of grade school, and when I went to live with Grandma I was transferred to a public Catholic school. I made my first communion in August of that year, and in February of the following year I was confirmed—what an experience. I was selected to be a member of the scholarship class, and at that time I set a goal to be a scholarship winner, an opportunity for a secondary education. Even at that early age, it was the guidance of the Holy Spirit in my life; however, at nine years old, I had no idea of this. Determination and hard work are traits I adopted in my formative years.

The scholarship class at that time was a concentration of studies geared to winning scholarships. We were segregated from the regular classwork and were tutored by the principal himself, on stage. When my mother returned home 2 1/2 years later, she came to collect her brood, but I was too busy to go home with her. Though I loved my mother dearly, my first priority was to get my scholarship, so I remained with my grandmother until I had written my qualifying competitive exam. I was so caught up with my own goal that nothing else mattered!

At this point, I did not realize that the Holy Spirit was desirous of changing my heart and my life. (I thought I was doing all these things on my own strength.) I know now that it was the Holy Spirit who took me from a Protestant environment and placed me in the Catholic community where I belonged. Now I know that without God's help I would not have been able to realize my dream. God, the guiding Force in my life then and now, gave me what I asked for. I also know that if I had asked God for something inappropriate, I would not have received it. Be careful what you ask for, because you just might get it.

ADOLESCENCE/CELIBACY

I did win a scholarship and spent six years in St. Joseph's Convent, where along with academic subjects, I was rigorously drilled in religion: rosaries, prayers, novenas, and more prayers. When I wrote my General Certificate of Education (GCE) exam, I decided I had had enough of school. I was so sure I had passed, but I failed miserably! Having decided not to return to school, I turned to other areas. God always has other plans for our lives. After graduation, I wanted to be a nurse. I applied at the General Hospital and was invited to write the entrance exam, which I expected to be hygiene and biology. The questions were general knowledge questions, and I did not qualify.

I had no idea how to cope with failure and went into a depression, but the Holy Spirit in healing my depression directed me into the commercial field. I enrolled in the local secretarial college. The courses required writing exams, and although I had become fearful about writing exams, passing those exams was confirmation of the healing power of the Holy Spirit. I believe it was the Holy Spirit who provided a job for me at the intermediate level of the program, and I completed the program through the adult evening classes.

It was shortly after I had reached the intermediate level that my mother became ill and needed nursing care for about six months. During that time, I was surrogate mother, housewife, and businesswoman—at age seventeen. Looking back at that period of my life, I ask myself, how could I have accomplished all this? The answer is simple; the Holy Spirit working in me gave me the strength to do what I had to do.

I had obtained study leave when my mother was ill, but one day when I was overcome by fatigue, I had a shower and lay down for what I thought would be a couple of minutes. The minutes stretched into four hours. Sleeping during the day is something I have always had trouble with, even now. If sleep occurs, I am physically ill; however, on that day, I was not ill. I had been fretting that my life was on permanent hold, and I wondered just how much longer I could go on. This incident showed my mother that she could resume control of her life gradually. This surely was divine intervention, because I could not say to my mother that it was time to make an effort to start taking over the reins as she was much better. God answers prayers in mysterious ways.

Two months after I resumed my course of study, I was offered my first job as a junior stenographer with a large department store. The only work I had done was in the variety store owned by my parents. As a junior stenographer, promotion and pay increases were awarded to me on merit and performance, without the benchmarks used in Canada. I received pay increases when salaries for other employees were frozen. I was a sponge for knowledge. After six months, I was chief stenographer, as the other two girls had left for higher-paying jobs in other companies.

At nineteen, I fell in love (or thought I was in love), a friendship that was to consume six years of my life. Again, the Holy Spirit guided me through my mother and other caring people. When I met him, Clifford, twelve years older than I, had left the seminary where he was studying to be an Anglican minister. He was very handsome, with the most beautiful blue eyes and a dimple in his chin, but from the beginning the friendship was plagued with conflict and pain because he liked girls. I was critical and uneasy all the time the friendship lasted; however, I continued to pray that God would give me the strength to resist his advances until we were married. It was during this friendship that I became aware of celibacy and how it would affect my life.

Celibacy for me means total abstinence, and I believe that means abstinence from everything. The Catholic Church teaches that sex is sinful outside of marriage. I abided by that teaching through fear of pregnancy. In our permissive society, it was the hardest thing I've ever had to do, and I know I was strong only because I prayed daily for the grace to be strong. Because I was confused about where the friendship was going, I asked God to tell me if I was meant to marry Clifford. The answer came in the form of an invitation to visit the Canadian Immigration Officer, scheduled to interview prospective immigrants. I invited Clifford to come along to the interview, as was suggested, and he said he wanted no part of my immigration plans. It was then I knew most definitely that the Holy Spirit was guiding me. The Holy Spirit really works, if we're tuned in. I know now that although I loved Cliff and he was good to me, I could not have lived with the thought of his infidelity.

The Holy Spirit also warns us of danger. I had a dream, a vision of Clifford breaking his arm. Normally, I never remember my dreams when

I awake, but this one was so powerful that I felt there was some significance to it. I saw him going out to work in the fields and having an accident; I watched him get hurt and was unable to help him. When I woke up, I was afraid. When I telephoned to warn him, his mother said he had left to make rounds at 8:15 that day. By midday, he did have a broken arm, and when he recounted the details of the accident, it was just as I had seen it.

It was about this time that the turning point came in my life, as I began to devote more time to prayer. Life in the Caribbean in the late sixties was glorious. As a single young adult, I had no social concerns and my life was uncluttered, untouched by tragedy. My faith was still fledgling but I pursued my goals relentlessly and succeeded because of the disciplines I set for myself. Changes must come, and I became restless for a new life. Though most of my friends were emigrating to England, I chose Canada, away from all relatives, for what was to become a difficult new start, learning to be really independent.

When I arrived in Toronto in October of 1965, my friends met me at Pearson International Airport and welcomed me to Canada and to my new life. I had no idea what it was like to live in an apartment, but I soon found out! In Canada I had to compete for jobs, whereas my first job was offered to me after a ten-minute interview with the managing director of Granby's Store in Grenada. In Canada, I had to fill out applications and take the required tests. I was offered two jobs at the same time and had to make a choice. I elected to work for Physicians Services Inc. to earn the required funds to enable me to attend school full-time while working towards an official secretarial diploma. After ten months at Shaw Business College, I had my Executive Secretarial Diploma with Honors! Later I was to attend university and get a bachelor of arts in sociology, and eighteen months later a Certificate in Personnel and Industrial Relations. A master's in sociology and a doctorate would be my next challenges.

UNDERSTANDING SPIRITUALITY

Spirituality has really strengthened me as an adult. During my maturing years, my faith in God was still conservative. The changes that evolved in the Roman Catholic Church after Vatican II caused much confusion in my spiritual life because I did not understand them. My belief has always been that if the Catholic Church is the true church, handed down by Christ, the changes should not be so drastic. My closeness with God, especially during Eucharist, was affected. So I did what everyone else does when conflict occurs, I took a Church vacation! After two years, I was ready to recommit myself, and here I am, more involved than ever!

I really answered the call and began to come to terms with my spirituality when my mother became ill with cancer. From all examinations and x-rays three weeks prior to being diagnosed, she was fine, but after noticing some disturbing symptoms, she visited the doctor. A series of tests confirmed medical suspicions. Surgery was performed, but her condition was so advanced that she was given six months to live. When I heard the news, I was furious, and I expressed all the anger I felt toward God. If I was so special, this should never happen to me! I laugh about it now; who was I to tell God what to do or to question God's motives? After my tirade, I became quite calm, even rational, and it was then I prayed as I had never prayed before. I remember asking God not to let my mother be in pain, as I had heard that that strain of cancer was very painful.

Be careful what you pray for; this was one of those successful "God answers prayers" stories. For the duration of her illness, my mother was never in pain and needed no morphine. Although she was asked repeatedly, "Are you in pain?", her answer always was, "No, I'm not in pain." She was upset at being constantly asked if she were in pain, but I knew and understood that God had spared her the pain as I had asked. This reaffirmed my conviction that the Holy Spirit does heed our prayer. Mother died in March 1982.

I was not involved in the renewal in the Roman Catholic Church, but from all events in my family around this time, I came to believe the Spirit works if we open our hearts. After my mother died, I continued to pray, but it was not always easy. My friend Ann said to me, "Trish, you've been through a lot this year. Why don't you come with me to the Catholic Women's League Convention in Prince Edward Island? It would be good for you, and you can have a nice little holiday." I agreed; I needed a holiday. The thought of attending a convention of which I was not a member was not of much interest to me, but Ann assured me that it was all right. When I attended the first session, I became so impressed with the warmth, spiritual richness, and friendliness of these women that I wanted to become a member at once! This was not just a chance encounter. God wanted me to become more involved in the Church, and Ann was the medium, involvement in the Catholic Women's League the method.

Sunday Mass had always been sufficient for me, but on the anniversary of my mother's death, I attended a Mass that I offered for the repose of her soul. At that time, morning Masses were at 8:15 A.M. I discovered that I could attend Mass and still get to work about the same time. I believe the Holy Spirit was inviting me to share Eucharist on a daily basis, and I said yes! I get such rich blessings now when I start my day with morning Mass that I consider it a privilege!

There is a lot to learn about spirituality, and it is a process that cannot be hurried. Every day I learn something new. One simple task that is very meaningful is to stop during the day to say, "God, I'm here, how am I doing today?" I am rewarded with a constant peace and joy deep within my heart. When I pray for the fruits of the Holy Spirit—love, joy, peace, patience, kindness, goodness, faithfulness, gentleness, and self-control—my prayers are always heard!

Everything becomes stronger when it is shared, even spirituality, so I joined a prayer group to enrich my spirituality. I soon learned that the path to the spiritual dimension is continual prayer. When I am not as prayerful as I should be, I get anxious, feel disturbed, and do not function peacefully. Jesus, when He was on earth, often went away to a lonely place to pray. He invites us to spend time with him, and a weekend retreat is a good way to spend time with God. The Catholic Church suggests that we make a retreat whenever possible; I do and it is the next thing to heaven. My spiritual life gives me a sense of well-being and keeps me calm in turbulent situations, which helps me to love God and to love my neighbor.

CONCLUSION

When I began my story, I said that I wanted to share the various events in my life that are the reasons for my deep spiritual commitment. I hope that you can see how the Spirit has used my faith, my parents, and other means to guide me along the path chosen for me.

All Catholics through their Baptism have the Holy Spirit with them; this is reaffirmed at our confirmation. If we can develop and identify our spirituality at an early age, we will be abundantly blessed. When we can put God first in our lives, life becomes a wonderful adventure! Sometimes it is a struggle, but the struggles occurred within me when I did not put God first. I have also found that struggles help me grow stronger spiritually. I trust God, I believe in God, and I love God!

Try loving God; you will enjoy a peace beyond understanding!

19 Living Out of the Center

Vicki Morgan

> I want a grounding in the solitary center of my being, beyond the hurt that undoes, in a grounding sufficiently certain that I do not get in the way of what I must be and do. It is a matter of not being easily undone—strength, serenity, confidence without the need of excessive and romantic hope.
>
> W. Paul Jones, *The Province Across the River*

When I was a child the year 2000 seemed way off in the future; I remember calculating I would be forty-two that year, which seemed old from my young perspective. I didn't know how my life would turn out, but I had planted fairly firmly in my little mind the vision of marriage and family. Through my twenties, my life felt generally full and meaningful—I traveled, did volunteer work with church-related organizations, and spent time off and on in my home state of Oregon catching my breath for the next adventure. The standard question was always, "How long are you home this time?" Although I had passing interests in a few potential relationships, I tried to not make a long-term relationship a focus for fear that it would preoccupy me in an unhealthy way. I felt undue orchestration on my part just wasn't necessary; if I followed what I sensed to be God's leading, I would be offered what I needed, and at some level, I hoped that would include marriage.

Planning to avoid a status quo sort of life-style, I nevertheless felt somewhat sure that by now I would be married to a one-of-a-kind renegade nice guy with 1.8 "birth" children and one or two adopted children to round out the family. I dreamed of living in a rural setting, tucked into the woods somewhere, becoming a self-sufficient "earth mama" who managed to balance the calls to nurture my own spiritual, emotional, and mental growth with the call and invitation to live responsibly and compassionately in the world. So when, at thirty-two, I encountered the man of my dreams—an earthy carpenter who loved to sing, dance, and play with children—I thought, "Ah, here's the person I've been waiting for all my life," not pining away for, just patiently (most of the time) waiting and watching. I felt I could trust his quiet way of being, his thoughtful listening. It seemed too good to be true, but I had waited a long time, and I felt I deserved this reward for my patience.

So I let myself enjoy it . . . for a time. As quickly as things seemed to come together, things fell apart. It had seemed so right, so timely, so full of potential for a long, full, meaningful life with someone I thought I could love well. I had invested myself emotionally to a degree that I could hardly see my way clear to dig myself out. Was I so stupid that I couldn't read the situation correctly? Had I become a victim of my romantic hopes (which weren't centered in genuine hope)? I had made a major mistake in judgment and I felt really stupid—I felt sad, indignant, mad, and just plain depressed. I felt rejected, abandoned, undone, by this seemingly sudden (not so sudden in retrospect) change of heart. I was preoccupied with this deep pain and felt lower than I'd ever felt before. I recognized that there was more at work than the disappointment of this lost love; there was a deeper sense of abandonment, a need to know that I was loved deeply and unconditionally.

During the time in which I was sorting through this pain, I began the process of making a decision as to whether or not I would join the community where I lived in Georgia. I missed my family in Oregon, but I had already invested so much in being in Georgia. Not only was the life in intentional community meaningful and rich but the Central American refugees with whom we worked and lived had touched my life deeply. Their stories of deep emotional pain, of torture, of being forced to leave family and homeland behind forced me to look at all of the things I took for granted: safety, family love and security, more than enough to eat, and relative political stability. As they shared their lives with me, I was drawn to pour myself more completely into their world. My first volunteer experience with the community was in 1985 when I spent nine months there. I left for a couple of years and in that time worked and saved enough money to travel to Central America to study Spanish and to experience firsthand as much as I could of the reality of those countries and their people. It was a meaningful six months, one of those times in my life when I felt I was fully awake to everything going on around me and within me. I returned to Georgia, realizing that the people of Central America had become part of me; I became more and more committed to their dreams for peace, for an end to the fear and distrust that had been so much a part of their lives. They showed me it was possible to laugh and dance—to celebrate—in the midst of their painful memories, the agonizing separations from family members.

Yet after nearly three years of sharing life in this community, I was faced with the possibility of leaving. Could I make that leap into the unknown? I had lived outside community, so I knew I could support myself, but it was facing the death of this dream of finding home and family in this place that really pained me. It felt as though the tablecloth had been pulled off this banquet table and had taken the banquet with it. I felt empty, and wondered if I had been so far off the mark in doing what I understood my "call" to be. Had I even been listening to God, or had I followed some unhealthy impulses that depended too much on outward response to who I was and the work I did?

I saw that maybe I had never really learned what it meant to live life from the center, although I felt I had long understood the idea and had perhaps even experienced it for periods of time. I began to wonder if I had ever known (in the sense of "in my bones") love. What did this strong fear of abandonment mean, if not a lack of trust or knowledge of God as Love? It wasn't as if I had never felt loved or appreciated, but I was beginning to question whether or not I was loved for exactly who I was apart from what I did. It had become unclear. But I knew that I was looking for love and security in a place, in a relationship, and in what I did; all of these things kept the focus outside myself. Life hadn't totally lost meaning—the arrival of lacy dogwoods still evoked a sense of wonder, I could still laugh and sing—but I spent a lot of time in tears, too. There was a thread of distrust, of anger, of deep brokenness that would surface in my thoughts and my actions. Clearly, I had become undone because I had lost my perspective. Looking for my primary security in relationship and in community, I had come up lacking, wanting still to be loved but knowing that I hadn't gone deep enough yet to find a Love and Presence that would sustain and free me. I knew somehow that the answers were beyond me and yet paradoxically within me. I began to see that intensely shared community life was not the place for me to sort this out. In spite of the fact that this work was good work and indeed the work of God, it was time for me to go.

The answer lay in Love, in losing myself in God to truly find myself. The answer lay in self-emptying, in being stripped of my attachments to all that was not God, of all that kept me from being a free person. I knew that unless I took the time to discover, to lay hold, to know the Love deeply, something in me would die . . . or at the very least, I would continue to shuffle through the motions of "doing" without a true-to-myself "being." It was an agonizing time. I had become far too dependent on the whims of approval and disapproval of those around me. Feeling immobilized in my pain, in feeling unloved, in not having a clear sense of direction in terms of vocation or home, I felt lost and confused. As in the beginning of I Corinthians 13, my love had been reduced to a clanging cymbal—my "doing" was out of a very broken sense of "being." I needed to recover a healthy sense of being—emotionally, spiritually, physically, and mentally. While I saw these dreams come apart I had a deep sense of the support of my family, although they were three thousand miles away. Friends offered the gift of their presence, of caring and confidence that deep inside me lay the answer to my pain. Growing up in the Quaker tradition, I had confidence that if I listened closely to the still, small voice I would know what it was that I needed to do. The Light was pretty faint, but I knew it was there.

I had taken a month of retreat time in Colorado at the Spiritual Life Institute's (SLI) Hermitage, a Catholic monastic community of men and women "apostolic hermits." It was a part of my process of decision making in considering whether or not I would pursue a long-term commitment to the community in Georgia. Out of that experience, the SLI community invited me to consider spending a longer time with them in their monastery in the wilderness of Nova Scotia. Something deep within me responded; somehow I knew that I needed to do exactly that, to remove myself from situations in which my sense of self depended on outward response or was defined by my "doing." Whether or not I could articulate it then, I sensed a drawing toward a way of looking at life and God that didn't put myself at the center, of self-forgetfulness.

I was drawn by the idea that it was possible to arrive at a place where I wasn't undone by circumstances, by my environment, by the response or lack of response to my ideas or to me as a person. Simply stated, I was looking for healthy self-love, for a deeper sense of worth and being loved that I somehow knew couldn't be met just by other people. I had become aware of my need to let go of my expectations, however subconscious, that my security lay in people and a place.

It was clear to me that this new season of my life was anything but an escape. Knowing that I'd be spending six months in the deep wilderness of Nova Scotia, many folks wondered if I was running away from my pain, but I knew I had to experience God by leaping into the unknown, into the Mystery. Living and working primarily alone appealed to me (not to mention the luxury of being beyond the reach of a telephone!), and the monastic rhythm would offer me a chance to be more deliberate about spiritual discipline, which I knew would be helpful in my desire to live out of the center. I recognized that not everyone could or even necessarily should take this step to retreat in the same way, nor does everyone have the emotional and financial support of friends and family. But it was clear I had to do this in response to this sense of call, of a hunger for a deeper, more committed life and as a response to God, to this loving, merciful, sometimes present, often seemingly absent Presence. I wanted to know in my gut that I wouldn't be abandoned, and somehow I knew I couldn't really know that without being alone, just God and me working it out. I knew from my experience in Colorado that the community life would be present and meaningful, but the life of the community members was one that pointed toward God dependence rather than people dependence; the community lived "together alone."

I knew this was a new threshold on my spiritual quest. It intrigued me and it terrified me—what would it really mean to let go? Would the unknown be less painful than the known? I had to plunge in . . . and I did. I had to explore and really live the idea that healthy "doing" springs from a sense of healthy "being." I hoped this could be the beginning of living differently. I wanted to continue living responsibly in terms of a compassionate life-style, cultivating my awareness of my role in the global scheme of things, and I wanted to do this in the context of a life that reflected a lack of self-preoccupation, a passion for wonder, for the simple everyday pleasures of life—enjoying a group of friends gathered around a fire on a lakeshore on an icy morning, glorying in the timeless call of a loon, gratefulness for the cheerful greeting of an urban bus driver, reconnecting with family too long separated. I wanted to live fully awake to the sacred that is at the heart of every act and our very existence.

Life at the Nova Scotia community was full of sacred, wild, "ordinary" moments. During my stay there I didn't want to waste my time in endless self-analysis but to acknowledge and even embrace my pain so that I could move through it and forgive people by whom I'd been hurt. I felt layers peeling away—just when I thought I'd accepted something or come to some resolution about an issue, it would hit me from a different angle. Asking for help has never been one of my strengths and so it was especially hard as my world fell apart around me in Georgia. It was difficult to ask for support when I needed it and at times just plain painful to acknowledge the depth of pain I felt. Why couldn't I just "get over it"?

In Nova Scotia I was challenged again by this reticence to admit my imperfections (the illusions run deep!), when I fell on the ice one day and injured my right hand severely enough that I couldn't use it to write, to haul water, even to chop vegetables. As I struggled to admit that I just couldn't do certain things, especially work-related tasks, it hit me full force: here I was again struggling to admit that I wasn't perfect, and this was a "mistake" over which I had no control! But I felt apologetic asking someone to draw the water from the well and carry it to my hermitage, I learned to chop vegetables left-handed and to type hunt-and-peck style with my left hand. Pride seemed to loom around every corner. I began to realize that learning to let go could and would be a life time process. Thomas Kelly in *A Testament of Devotion* reminded me that gritting my teeth wouldn't help; I needed to accept that I'm not perfect (an illusion of self-sufficiency that has plagued me for a long time) and to be gentle with myself in this painful, bittersweet process of becoming human. There are many times when I feel like I'm more darkness than light and times when my actions fall so short of my ideals. I become so easily disappointed in myself but I do hope that I can make healthy choices that move me toward greater wholeness and deeper transformation, and I hope to have some fun in the process—to be light more than darkness.

After living with other people all my life (family, roommates, communities), I've chosen to live alone for the time being, to work part-time and to live close to my family in order to nurture more deliberately those relationships that have been primarily long-distance for the last twelve years or so. Sometimes I struggle with the limitations brought about by choosing to live this way—the limited income, the bite out of my check for rent (probably twice as much as in a shared living arrangement), not having my own car—but there are opportunities with these choices as well. I generally have time for reading, for quiet and prayer, for exercise and creative activities before I have to be at work. I've been able to take classes and hope to be more deliberate about using some of my mornings for volunteer work. I also have a fair amount of flexibility in spending time with family and friends.

Although I'm still drawn to intentional community as a life-style, I feel confident that it's good for me to spend time with more autonomy. This autonomy, this time of being alone, used well, can be exhilarating, empowering; used badly, it becomes a lonely, frustrating existence. Spending time meditating, journaling, and walking meditatively all help me to focus. I try to be purposeful about spending Sunday in a Sabbath mode, putting aside responsibilities in order to enter into this sanctuary in time as Abraham Heschel emphasizes in his eloquent book *The Sabbath*. Following in the pattern of the monks in Nova Scotia, I take seriously the mandate as stated in their brochure to "waste the day [Sunday] by praying and playing."

I'm still in the process of settling into a faith/worship commmunity and hope to establish a connection with someone for spiritual direction to further direct me on this journey; it's clear that I can't do it alone, and I'm convinced that it's a great gift we offer each other when we share the Light we have on this stumbling, fumbling, sometimes glorious quest to be "oned" with God. In Brendan Doyle's *Meditations with Julian of Norwich*, Julian's timeless wisdom comes through:

Until I am really and truly oned and fastened to God so that there is nothing created between us, I will never have full rest or complete happiness. . . . We seek rest where there is no rest and therefore are uneasy. God is the True Rest who wants to be known. God finds pleasure in being our true resting place. (26)

So one of my creative tensions is to live with my dreams, longings, and expectations for my own growth in the future while being present and available to what it is I'm offered in the here and now. I've come to a place where I try to hold my dreams lightly—to not be afraid to dream but to do so in a detached way, knowing that life is a gift and that if I trust the Love that's at the heart of the universe, my deepest needs will be met. It has meant struggling with my fears of what it means to really say yes to God, but I'm beginning to believe that my freedom ultimately lies in this letting go, this dying to self.

Frequent paradox hits me in this struggle; how can I admit and even fearlessly embrace these longings, these dreams and not lose sight of the wonder, of the beauty, of the opportunity of the present? Kelly's *A Testament of Devotion* reminds us that everything we need is present in the "Eternal Now" (95). My hope is that I'll approach every task or encounter with another person as an opportunity to encounter this sacredness. Sometimes I'm half asleep, muddling through a task or conversation with my mind on other things—I don't taste that juicy drippin'-down-my-chin peach, I don't hear those words of excitement or pain—I am not open to the miracle of that particular moment, and so I miss the experience of the incredible juicy peach or am too asleep to encounter "that of God" which is present in everyone. Thus the most ordinary encounters and simplest tasks can become sacred acts, reminders of God's presence in the everyday. The importance of doing things mindfully can change how I look at an otherwise "boring" task. Brother Lawrence, a Carmelite monk, as well as many "ordinary" folks, have found tasks such as washing dishes to be holy, times of experiencing a deep sense of God's presence. But to be aware of this sacredness means waking up, listening carefully, focusing on the task, putting all your energy into the present moment.

Another way in which I've been half awake is to live, in a sense, a derivative existence through my tendency to live through other people, to lett others determine my reality, to put too much effort into "pleasing all the people all of the time"—and then to be bitterly disappointed when I've fallen short of my expectations or those of other people. Thus I've been only half awake to the deeper call to live out of the center, to be surrendered to the deepest reality, God. It means believing and living in such a way that I acknowledge that I am loved unconditionally. But it's not a matter of just saying I am loved; it has to go beyond intellectual knowledge, which is a process that mystifies me. How is it that one moment I have knowledge about this Love, and then I find myself overwhelmed with really experiencing this Love? Accepting this Love has enabled me to trust God more readily, to trust and accept what the present offers, not to get bogged down in the past or the future. Blaise Pascal presents a thought-provoking reflection in *Pensées*:

> We do not rest satisfied with the present. We anticipate the future as too slow in coming, as if in order to hasten its course; or we recall the past, to stop its too rapid flight. So imprudent are we that we wander in the times which are not ours, and do not think of the only one which belongs to us; and so idle are we that we dream of those times which are no more, and thoughtlessly overlook that which alone exists, for the present is generally painful to us. We conceal it from our sight, because it troubles us; and if it be delightful to us, we regret to see it pass away. We try to sustain it by the future, and think of arranging matters which are not in our power, for a time which we have no certainty of reaching.
>
> Let each one examine his thought, and he will find them all occupied with the past and the future. We scarcely ever think of the present; and if we think of it, it is only to take light from it to arrange the future. The present is never our end. The past and the present are our means; the future alone is our end. So we never live, but we hope to live; and, as we are always preparing to be happy, it is inevitable we should never be so. (#172)

Life lived from the center is life lived without regrets and, one hopes, with a minimum of fear. It means letting go of all the times I've really blown it—it means believing that I am changing, that I'm moving up a spiral and not just in circles. It means waiting, but it also means acting in response to what I hear in the prompting of the Spirit. In fear I sometimes respond to that voice with talk, with reading a mindless book, or with radio noise. A woman I met while I was on retreat in Nova Scotia mentioned that fear always reflects living in the past or in the future; of course fear is a natural response to threat, but when it becomes the very thing that motivates me or keeps me from acting, I've slipped out of the mode of being "present in the present." I sometimes live in regret of not doing something when I finally experience something, such as a swim in the still, golden lake at 5:30 A.M.—bliss. I'll say, "Why didn't I do this before?" instead of appreciating the fact that it finally dawned on me to do it. So I've decided to turn an overused saying on its head: live not as if "today is the first day of the rest of your life," but live with the passionate response of someone who has just discovered that "today might be the last day of your life." I hope to live more passionately, to be more available and receptive, more open to what's happening in me, around me, and in the world, and more awake to the gratefulness that is at the heart of existence and at the "heart of prayer," as Brother David Steindl-Rast so beautifully explains in *Gratefulness, the Heart of Prayer*.

Centered living implies self-knowledge, but in my own searching I've found that sometimes the searching that accompanies the quest to find that elusive self can be twisted into self-preoccupation. My thoughts become easily scattered as I remember the pain of rejection, a battle of the wills in which I was clearly wrong. Often these musings into the past are on incidents that occurred many months or even years ago, so such thoughts are clearly wasted energy, and the incidents need to be forgiven and let go.

In the words of Father William McNamara of the Spiritual Life Institute, the cultivation of the virtue of humility is "not to think little of ourselves but to think of ourselves very little." Other definitions imply that humility calls for honesty about ourselves, in essence celebrating the light and the shadow that reflect who we are.

This searching is a movement toward wholeness as I come to accept myself in process. This movement toward becoming fully human is the process that draws us into the Holy Other. More and more I appreciate words that can only reflect the Mystery that is God, words that fall short of wrapping themselves around the Being of God but express some attempt to describe and give name to the many-faceted Spirit in whom we "live and move and have our being," the Spirit which is both within and beyond me.

Being centered is to live out of the deep connectedness of all of life. I have been told that author Madeleine L'Engle eloquently states that when a butterfly moves its wings, the world is somehow changed. Thus every act of love, and of violence, has repercussions. Every word, unkind or encouraging, ripples through time. At a seminar in which many peace activists were present, Father Thomas Keating, a Trappist monk, was asked how he would define a peacemaker. It was clear that the questioner wanted Keating to encourage everyone to voice their protests in a particular way, to perhaps take to the streets communicating their hopes, their dreams, and their deep disagreements with current social or political policy, in other words, to deal with social problems and lack of justice and peace in a way that might bring policy change on a large scale. His reply didn't contradict these as possible options, but he went further. He was firm but gentle: "A peacemaker is anyone who brings healing into our world."

We can hope for change; our prayers, our faithful and compassionate actions, our life-style choices, our "standing with" oppressed peoples, our letters to Congresspeople and to other power brokers, do affect the cosmos whether or not we see the direct results. Our way of being affects the world. There is a ripple effect. Our job is to be faithful to our task, to look at God's will as something that manifests itself in our actions as we become exactly who we are meant to be: integrated, celebrative, humble, exuberant, single-minded, Light-bearing people. We can then act with integrity and clarity.

I've long been comforted by Thomas Kelly's words in *A Testament of Devotion* about not needing to respond to every need: "The Loving Presence does not burden us equally with all things, but considerately puts upon each of us just a few central tasks, as emphatic responsibilities. For each of us these special undertakings are our share in the joyous burdens of love" (109). When I find myself confused with conflicting options or directions, I count on the wisdom of my family or close friends. Within the Friends tradition is the option for a "meeting for clearness" in which people prayerfully gather to discern the mind of God. This process of discernment, of active listening and waiting can be a very affirming and clarifying time.

I see the need for this patient waiting in my own journey, in relationships, and in situations of injustice. Within the waiting I may be prompted to take action, and I want to be obedient to that call, but my response is often more likely to be a scattered and untimely action that reflects my impatience. Nikos Kazantzakis illustrates the importance of patience in the process of transformation in *Zorba the Greek*:

I remembered one morning when I discovered a cocoon in the bark of a tree, just as the butterfly was making a hole in its case and preparing to come out. I waited a while, but it was too long appearing and I was impatient. I bent over it and breathed on it to warm it. I warmed it as quickly as I could and the miracle began to happen before my eyes, faster than life. The case opened, the butterfly started slowly crawling out and I shall never forget my horror when I saw how its wings were folded back and crumpled; the wretched butterfly tried with its whole trembling body to unfold them. Bending over it, I tried to help it with my breath. In vain. It needed to be hatched out patiently and the unfolding of the wings should be a gradual process in the sun. Now it was too late. My breath had forced the butterfly to appear, all crumpled, before its time. It struggled desperately and, a few seconds later, died in the palm of my hand. That little body is, I do believe, the greatest weight I have on my conscience. For I realize today that it is a mortal sin to violate the great laws of nature. We should not hurry, we should not be impatient, but we should confidently obey the eternal rhythm. (138–139)

It is in active listening and in patient waiting on God that our rest lies. Freedom lies in the realization that I am loved at the center of my being, that I am free only when I am detached from everything that points me away from Love, from those things that keep me from moving toward deeper wholeness and joy. As the monks in Nova Scotia say, a balance of deep prayer and exuberant play is essential. This focus (or goal) doesn't mean I can hide behind being prayerful as a way to remove myself from the world, nor does a playful attitude mean irresponsible action. Contemplation is a way of seeing, of "taking a long, loving look at the Real," as Father William would say. It takes me to the heart of all things and thus connects me with the universal pain in a way that nothing else can, but it also compels me to act, to respond to that Love, to that dance, to that Presence in an act of love. I cannot remain passive and inactive if my life is grounded in prayer and active listening and waiting. Love at the center of my being demands a response—availability, service, action. And because perfect love casts out fear, if I'm living in recognition of that Love, I will have the courage to act. Kelly states: "[God] asks all but . . . gives all" (50).

As Kelly further explains, "The life that intends to be wholly obedient, wholly submissive, wholly listening, is astonishing in its completeness. Its joys are ravishing, its peace profound, its humility the deepest, its power world-shaking, its love enveloping, its simplicity that of a trusting child" (54).

VII Rebirthing in the Single Life

Many of the most difficult life changes are thrust upon us. Often amidst their grief and pain, we discover the essence of life. Rebirth involves giving up and renewing, death and resurrection.

"Single Again: On Emotional Recovery" is an eloquent account by Esly Regina Carvalho, of South America, in which the shock and loss of divorce prove to be preparation to help others face loss through war and natural disaster.

In "Of Wells," the story of Hagar and Ishmael in poetic form, Mabel Murray writes of her search for identity and spirituality after leaving her community of thirty-four years.

Describing the traumatic experience of early widowhood in India, Beulah Jeyaseeli strikes numerous universal chords. That she views her widowhood as a vehicle for God's purpose in her life is testimony that her faith has carried her through.

20 Single Again: On Emotional Recovery

Esly Regina Carvalho

Having the opportunity to write on this subject after my divorce seven years ago has given me a unique chance to reflect on and organize some of the experiences that I went through as God brought me closer to wholeness. It was a relatively simple process but certainly not an easy one. Today I can honestly say that life is full of unexpected turns in the road but that we can learn to greet these surprises as growing exercises and not something that will utterly destroy us.

ON LOSS

My marriage had been going downhill at a brisk pace by the time my daughter turned two. Less than a year later it was over. This was a terrible time in my life, a time of many losses. I had never thought about how much one loses in a divorce until they began to arrive. I lost my husband (obviously) and my marital status. I also lost his daughter by his first marriage, who had come to live with us after the birth of our child. She was twelve by then and had become an integral part of my life. I had to leave the house we had lived in, the neighborhood, and those friends who had surrounded us in so many ways. A month after my husband left I discovered I was pregnant, and with the discovery came a miscarriage and all of the conflicting feelings related to that experience. Having refused to consider an abortion (besides, it is illegal in Brazil), I lost the baby before I ever really made the adjustment to maternity. And yet, when I saw my best friend wearing maternity clothes that I had given her months before, I burst into tears . . .

Even the dog died. It was a time of death and dying.

Ecclesiastes speaks of a time to live and a time to die (Eccles. 3). This was certainly my time of death. So much died, but much more died within me. When I left the hospital after the miscarriage I realized that the love I had had for my husband had died with the baby. My hopes for a reconciliation were also dead after that. I didn't want the marriage to recover, and I prepared to confront life alone.

If there was one emotion that defined this period of my life, it was ambivalence. Ambivalence about the situation that I found myself in, toward my husband, my friends, my church, and toward God.

Back then, I wasn't certain that I could ever be comfortable with the idea of being a divorced woman. It wasn't a role I had ever intended to learn, and it went against so much of what I had wanted for myself and expected out of my life. But I had to admit that it was certainly here to stay, whether I wanted it or not. On the other hand, the relief that was offered by the separation had something to be said for it. In the last months of my marriage, there was so much fear present that not having to be so constantly afraid was a definite improvement. It was a fragile relief, almost like a respite, yet I could see that perhaps one day it could even be turned into a lasting peace instead of a temporary truce.

My feelings toward my husband were also very ambivalent. How could I hate and fear someone with whom I had fallen in love and had promised to love and cherish forever? I had had a child with this man, such a special experience, and now she had become one more bone of contention. How could I be so mad at him? Yet I knew that he was still important to me. My well-meaning friends would sometimes poke fun at me, implying that I still loved him. At first, I would defiantly deny it. With time, I owned up to the fact that it was very difficult to cut someone who had been so important to me out of my life at the drop of a hat. I understood that a divorce meant reversing the direction of intimacy; when we were first married, we worked at developing intimacy. With the separation, I was going to have to work at making this partner become a stranger again.

I was also ambivalent with my friends and toward my church. I knew that I certainly needed them, but I was very much aware that I had to risk their rejection to gain their support. I was very blessed in this period of my life by some special people who saw me through it all. One fine Christian woman prayed me through the difficult weeks and months that ensued. She has earned my eternal gratitude for her listening and her prayers. I am sure that I bored her to tears, yet she held in there and let me lean on her as I needed it.

Other people helped. One pastor would call every two weeks and leave a little message on my answering machine just to let me know that he was thinking of me and that if I should need him, I should please call. I still remember that with gratefulness. There was also a small church that took me in. Nobody asked any snoopy questions, yet I knew that I could ask the members to pray with me and that they would stand with me. The divorce changed nothing in our care for each other. I realize now that it was an added blessing.

The losses were tremendous. No wonder I always felt that my stores of energy had been depleted. I understood that I was working through these losses. I often let myself cry when I felt overwhelmed. It didn't solve any problems, but I felt better afterwards. Years later, when I began to work in Latin America training facilitators in emotional recovery in the face of great losses resulting from natural (and "unnatural") disasters (earthquakes, wars, civil strife, landslides), I perceived that God had guided my steps through my own process. Intuitively (or was it through the Holy Spirit?) I had given myself permission to feel the enormity of my losses and mourn them. There are no funerals for divorce or any other adequate or socially accepted rituals to mourn it. On the contrary, divorce is often whispered about in woeful tones of pity as if it were something shameful or disgraceful. Crying is a healing part of recovery, and I often saw that my patients who didn't cry their losses took much longer to recover and had to be encouraged to do so.

I was still very much afraid of rejection. I didn't get involved in church programs, went to very few meetings, spoke little, hoping to pass by unnoticed and thereby accepted.

Most of all, I was ambivalent toward God. I really couldn't understand how a God of love, harmony, and reconciliation was letting my marriage come crashing down around my ears. I thought it was up to God to keep it together, not to let it fall apart. I was upset with God for a good while, and yet I needed the Holy Spirit so desperately: for comfort, wisdom, consolation, and hope. God was my all and all, and in God's arms I often cried myself to sleep.

Many people had commented on how God had helped them through the more difficult parts of life. Now it was my turn to realize the reality of God's presence. There were so many things with which I felt that I couldn't cope. Simple things were a horrendous effort when I had to do it all in the midst of an unmeasurable depression. But I began to find God faithful in a new way. The money for the rent always came in. The patient load at the office increased without any effort on my part. And we had peace at home.

I spent one year mourning my losses. Life was always grey. I laughed very little. My ex-husband and I cried over the phone at Christmas when we recalled that the little baby should have been born about then.

And then, one day, life began to recover its colors.

CONVALESCENCE

In part, the process of convalescence began side by side with the mourning, but it was so infinitely difficult to see it that only when the loss had been properly worked through did I understand that it had begun much earlier.

This was the healing phase, the "let's get on with life" time. It was hard to mend what had been broken, salvage the good, and toss out what was worthless. It also had its humps, but good things began to come out of the pain. Six months after the divorce was finalized, I heard my daughter laugh her delicious giggle for the first time since the separation. I cried because I realized how long it had been since I had heard it, but I heard it and I knew that her winter snow was beginning to melt.

I spent a lot of time thinking during this period, perhaps even more talking it out. I did some therapy, which helped. I prayed that God would change me so I wouldn't make the same mistakes again. I made monumental decisions that have had consequences into the present and for which I am grateful. I decided to make the best life possible for my daughter and me. We were a family, reorganized, nontraditional, but a family. We were going to have a home, not a house. God was going to be the head of the household, the father, the husband. I read Proverbs 31:10 until I could recite it by heart: "Who says only married women are 'virtuous'?"

Virtue was not something I figured I derived from my civil state. So I tried to write my first book but had to stop halfway because of the emotional hemorrhage. I wasn't well enough to finish, but I was well enough to start.

I began to go out and do things. I started my master's degree. Knowing how hard I could be on myself, I made a promise to start but to stop when I felt that I couldn't go on or when my daughter needed me more than the books. (They kept me company on the weekends she was off with her dad. It also helped ease the pain of the empty bedroom. She was only four.) I graduated three years later with a thesis on family structure.

I made new friends. I hung on to some of my married friends, but they usually had different schedules, lived far away, or had moved on to other things. Some of them backed away from me, but in most cases, the friendships simply lost their meaningfulness. Other friends had been "his" to begin with.

I discovered I had a new freedom to come and go. Some days I felt more married than single, such as when I had my daughter with me, needed a babysitter, couldn't find a place to leave her after school so that I could keep on working. But other times, I was "single again," and I had never thought that the solitude could become company. I began to like being alone. I discovered it didn't necessarily mean loneliness. It was a fun time, and I began to appreciate my own company, but in small doses initially. I couldn't take it all at once. I would read a book, listen to the music I liked, eat when I felt like it, do my papers for school, or sleep in the middle of the afternoon (more and more out of tiredness and less and less out of depression). When I got tired of myself, I'd call a friend and go out somewhere.

Life began to bloom in new colors.

MOVING ON

As life began to take on new colors, so did I. I wore red, not black; bright green, not dead grays. Life was beginning to get interesting, and each day brought new challenges and not just another chapter in the Survivor's Manual of Life. I was beginning to realize that there was life after divorce.

Most intriguing, I realized that it was a great life, and surviving was not all there was to it. Perhaps because I also became a more interesting person, I was invited to do things I had never done before. As I thrilled in the new challenges, I transmitted the sheer and utter enjoyment that I got out of it. People, in turn, began to give me new challenges. I received my first invitation to teach abroad—in another language! I accepted it, and the folks helped me stumble through my Spanish. (I already spoke Portuguese.) They were patient with me since they felt that I really had something to contribute. Years later, many of those patient students became the founding members of the first Psychodrama Association in Ecuador.

I was sent to Nicaragua in January 1989. My heart broke over the suffering the war and the tornadoes had wrought. I shed many tears with the mothers whose sons had been lost defending their country against the war of aggression. I was humbled by the prayers that blessed the food we ate. Truly these were holy meals. These people prayed gratefully, some of them absolutely certain that they did not know where their next meal was coming from, thankful that they had this one. I fell in love with them, and in the geography of my heart, you will find a special place for the "Nicas."

Ironically, I discovered I was especially equipped to teach emotional recovery. I had come through. I knew it could be done.

The other children I never had, have become new endeavors. I went into the "reproduction mode" by writing books and articles, slowly at first, later with more confidence. I "gave birth" to new lives in the consulting room. It happened before my eyes because I believed these people could do it. And I believed because spring had at last come knocking on my own door.

In the beginning of the convalescence period, I was constantly thinking of when I would remarry, how this would happen. Each new male who came into my life was eyed as a potential Prince Charming. As I recovered, I saw it for what it was: pure foolishness. I could not depend on the existence of another person in my life to bring me fulfillment. What if Prince Charming never arrived and I spent a lifetime treading water, "waiting for Godot"? Once this was settled, I could be friends with everyone. In truth, as time went on and my life got more exciting, I doubted that a relationship could enrich my life even more. I remained open to it (avoiding the familiar belief that "men are all alike—none of them are worthy to be trusted"), but I quit chasing it down. That was a big step.

I remembered that God had called me into the ministry of reconciliation when I was seventeen. God is faithful and brought that ministry into fruition in these years since my divorce. Life has never been better. As a matter of fact, I could never have imagined that it could be this good without marriage. I have had the chance to travel through Latin America and learn a new language. I have new friends who have different habits and customs. I have been ushered into the heartfelt intimacy of the people who populate my continent. What a privilege! I have been loved, appreciated, and recognized for my efforts. (I have also been criticized and had a few rocks thrown at me, but I discovered that I can take that, too.) Better yet, I have learned to love others better and to comprehend a new dimension of the mercy of God.

My daughter and I are closer than we have ever been now that sorrow no longer silences us. There is no shame to being a reorganized family—just "differentness." God is ever present in our lives. We turn to God because there is now a relationship of deep-felt trust. Having faced so many other difficult moments in the past, when the invitation to move to Ecuador came through last year, my daughter took up the challenge with me. Why not? We had overcome even tougher hurdles together.

My relationship with God has deepened, and the trust has reached a new level. Things don't have to go my way for me to maintain my friendship with God. I have discovered another side of the Almighty—what Leonardo Boff, my countryman, would call "the maternal face of God." I started work on a new book, one of poems: *Prayers to Mother God*. I know that this one I will be able to finish.

Finally, I have perceived that Paul was right—when we are weak, then we are strong. Out of my greatest weaknesses and anguish have come my greatest blessings and strengths. Or as Ernest Hemingway is quoted by Selwyn Hughes as having once put it, "Life breaks us all . . . but some of us become strong in the broken places" (1984, 1). God has made me strong in my broken places.

21 Of Wells

Mabel A. Murray

I am called Hagar.
My child is sitting under a bush.
I have put my child there, separate
from myself.
I feel the child shall die.
I shall die.

We are in the desert. Outcast.
I cry. The God I knew sent me from
camp,
from the familiar,
from the secure,
from the pain I could handle.

What is out here for the child?
What is out here for me?
Endless days of waste. And death.
I cry. My child is crying.

I set the child there. I put aside
the playful,
the serene,
the creative,
the trusting,
while I search for answers, for water,
for reasons.

I could have stayed in camp. My child is as chosen as Sarah's. My child is seed of Abraham.

I know his secrets. In the night he spoke of stars and sand and progeny.

His progeny is under a bush. In the sand, of the sand, like sand. Sand. Outcast. For no use. My child and I are one with the sand.

Stars. There are a multitude of stars. What promise is this? What good the whisperings of multitudes and presence?

Where are you, God of Abraham, Calling-God, Promising-God? You called me once. Call me again. My child is crying. Listen to my child.

Silence.
The silence of the desert begins. Winds whip the sand around me. Sand. The children I shall never see. Sand. The children my child shall never see.

The stars are cold and distant. No longer do they dance with images of greatness and power.

The Child Part 1

I am called Ishmael, the child. My mother sits far from me, rocking. She bends in sorrow.

I am frightened. My mother has always been close to me. Why is she away now?
Where is Isaac?
Where is Abraham?
Why am I here?
What has happened?
Food for the journey, our desert bread, is gone. Water, our water in the desert, is gone.
If Mother would look, she would find something. Why is she crying?
Mother, come. I am cold. I am afraid. Night is coming. Desert night is very dark. Mother, come. I'm calling.

* * * * *

My child sleeps. I watch over the youngster, my child. I embrace my child. I am one with my child. I am one my child can trust. I rock my child and croon old lullabies. All beyond is silence.

My child's body warms me in the night. Babyhood memories return. I feel blessed to have this child. Promises or no promises, we are together. Rejected by Abraham, by Abraham's God, we are together. And together, we shall sleep.

Sleep in the silence. Sleep in the barrenness. Sleep abandoned. But sleep together.

I shall make plans to get food and drink. Together we shall survive.

"Hagar."

The wind.

"Hagar."

I know that voice.

"Hagar."

Something stirs within me, like new life. Dare I hope? Yes, I know that voice.

I comfort my sleeping child and rise to respond. "Yes."

I am to go back. Back to camp. Back to Abraham. Back to security.

"Hagar."

The sound of the voice. The sound of knowing. Music. Water-music. I hear water. A well. I see it. A message? For my child? The child shall prosper? The God of Abraham shall be with my child?

Abraham's God who hears, who sees me, has seen me again. I go to my child.

We live! Praise be to you, God of the Universe, the one who sees. Once again I have seen you, My God. You are now my Water, my Provider, my Way in the desert.

Come, child. See what Abraham's God has done. Drink. Drink.

My child has grown away from me. I no longer feel the presence of play, of creativity, of trust.

In silence and solitude I walk the desert sand.

I am alone. No camp. No plan. No leader.

I walk the uncharted. The well is behind me now. I am left with a promise. A promise for my child. The child I no longer know. My child will be blessed. The God of Abraham will be with my child. So be it. But when?

I will look for another well.

I come to Isaac's waiting-well; waiting-to-see-what-happens-well. A well where love is found. Human love. Friendships, vast and satisfying. I pray with Isaac, Blessed be Yahweh, God of Abraham, for not stopping showing me kindness.

I stay and drink of this well. Then, in the midst of plenty, the desert thirst returns. The thirst like that of the sand. The thirst which an oasis fails to quench.

I will slake that thirst at the well of my ancestors. I know the way. Back to the God-well of my parents; back to the family-well, back to the hometown-well. I need root-water, parent-water, family-water, ancestral-water. I shall go back there. Maybe to be young again. Maybe to choose another path. The land is familiar. The well is near. Silence awaits me where once there was water-music. Closer and closer I come. Greater and greater is the silence of the well. I am there. Sand. Sand. All the way to the top. Sand. My mother's God is buried. My town is buried. My family is under sand. The music is stilled.

Without water, I begin to listen to the promise. I lived with water and a promise. I can live with a promise.

Darkness hovers over my path. No sound. No memory of the promise. Silence. Silence and darkness.

Wait. Wait for the dawn. Light will come with the dawn. Surely there will be a sign, an idea, hope.

The sun fails to rise.

Darkness remains.

Darkness and silence.

No stars.

Sand.

But no stars.

Darkness is my companion.

Silence, my guide.

Very well. There are other wells. These wells have water. I search them out. Yes, water. Muddied, unpalatable. Water, nevertheless. But, no music. I settle for conflict, for confusion, for brackish water.

Winds come. My tent is torn away. No camp. In the storm I have lost my way. I have lost the water. I have lost the bitterness, confusion and strife.

Darkness remains.

Silence remains.

Loyal companions. They are not water. But they are loyal. I can count on them. I can count on darkness. I can count on silence. Darkness and silence are like the desert. Present.

I begin to learn the language of the desert. I begin to learn the language of silence, of darkness.

There is a certain familiarity about that language. A word here and there. Play . . . be with . . . A language which begins to describe my child.

I begin to remember my child. Total, resting, trust. Abandon. Peace.

I look into the well of darkness, listening.

I look into the well of silence, listening.

I begin to realize that silence and darkness have dug a way, have dug an opening.

Darkness and silence have dredged into the depths of my being; into my desert; into my sand.

And in the darkness, the silence is broken. I hear music.

My heart responds. Something stirs.

Water.

Yes.

Water-music.

Within me.

Laughter fills the water-music. My child! I understand the language.

Darkness remains. Darkness, the music, and my child. Will this be the water to quench the desert thirst? Will this be the spring inside welling up to eternal life?

In darkness, I let down rope.

The Child Part 2

I am carefree.

I play again.

I trust. I create. I laugh. I lean
against my mother. There is peace.

I have been found,
       owned,
       rocked,
       and cherished.

I am growing. Growing in grace.

Growing in wisdom
     before Abraham's God,
     before all.
I play again.
I trust again.
I laugh again.
I lean against my mother.
Peace.

22 Widowhood: A Door of Hope

Beulah Jeyaseeli

The midsummer day dawned cheerfully as I made my entry into the world in a Lutheran pastor's family. I was raised in Christian nurture and have always known that I, like my other siblings, belong to Christ. But my wise grandmother, who combined the mysticism of the East with the gifts of the Holy Spirit, insisted that I was to be different. She told me that like some illustrious men of God in the Bible, I was named before my birth, that God specifically had told her to instruct my parents to call me Beulah; she said that Beulah means "married" and I was to be God's exclusively.

It was not difficult for an Indian girl to appreciate the prestige that went with the title "Married Woman"—*Sumangali,* the Indian's special word for it. Every Indian girl is forever wished by her elders on every occasion that she should be a *Sumangali*. In Indian society, the married woman is an auspicious omen, a benevolent force, and only the *Sumangali* can perform certain rituals during marriages and other special occasions. So I grew up assuming I would have this special status. This made me a radiant bride, very sure of my good fortune.

Even before the bridal glow faded, my husband had to be rushed for an emergency operation for a brain tumor that turned out to be malignant.

In spite of my dazed condition, I knew that God would not let me become a widow within a month of my marriage, particularly when it was God who had named me Beulah. But the wordly-wise matrons around me whispered that I had the malevolent influence of Saturn in my horoscope. It is a common belief that if a girl has the taint of Saturn, she will become a widow soon. They could very well have said Satan instead of Saturn. I was the criminal, and there was no appeal against this verdict.

So I directed all my fury toward God. "Why did you make a mockery of my name? Why saddle me with such a misnomer?" Then I dared God to take away my husband's life. God spared his life for three years, though he became totally blind; that was the least of our troubles.

I now had to fend for myself and support my invalid husband! I went back to teaching and in the three years, God wonderfully prepared me to accept my imminent widowhood. Seeing my husband's sufferings, finally I was forced to pray, "God take him, only spare him the agony." On the second birthday of our daughter, whom he had not "seen" with his eyes, he went into a coma and died seven days later.

Though I had been expecting this, my faith was shaken. Life seemed one long bitter struggle between unequal opponents. The world around me said, "It is your fate." If that were so, who decided my fate? Am I a puppet on a string in the hands of a capricious fate, or am I in the hands of a loving God who, in wisdom, has ordained such a map of my life? Is there such a thing as eternal life? Have I believed in vain? The questions were numerous, and I did not seem to have any answers.

Then one sultry afternoon I was teaching my biology class the life cycle of the amoeba. I told the class in a matter-of-fact tone that the amoeba perpetuated itself through binary fission and that it does not die unless it is deliberately destroyed. In a sense, it is eternal. Then suddenly but clearly I heard the challenge.

"So you believe that the amoeba, the lowest organism in God's creation, does not die, but you assume that humans, made in the likeness of God, disintegrate into dust simply because they cease to breathe?" This hit me like a thunderbolt.

I reasoned that since my daughter started her life with a speck of her father's protoplasm, he exists through her. But the euphoria did not last long. "What if she dies? After all, she is not a very robust child!" mocked the Tempter within me. I became almost paranoid about her health, and she had one sickness after another. I had no peace till I could say, "All right, God, I surrender my daughter, myself, and my flickering faith!" I think that was a major victory and the very foundation of my spirituality. Though I was not able to challenge, "O Death, where is thy sting?" (1 Cor. 15:55), I could at least look beyond the grave.

After this, God enabled me to analyze the parameters of my faith. Hadn't I been basing my faith on an invisible God on the evidence of material things? Wasn't I limiting the Immortal to mortal events? I examined some of the milestones of my trust-life.

I remembered the occasion when I was thirteen and had prayed for a pair of high heels. My opponent during the School Pupil Leader's election pointed out that I was quite short. I wanted instant increase in height and prayed for the loftier perch of a pair of high heels. It was answered miraculously. A long-lost uncle brought from Delhi a pair of high heels. I was astounded. I trusted God, like Gideon (Judg. 6) because I had physical evidence. (I still wish I had prayed for a taller figure.)

Then I recalled the days when my husband and I had prayed for the gift of life. It was answered partially. Contrary to medical expectation, he survived for three years, the years that gave us the gift of a daughter. I crossed the second milestone—of trusting God even when everything is bleak, as was the case with Paul during his tempestuous voyage (Acts 27:20–25).

The next mile was more arduous. One by one, God removed my props—my beloved father, my father-in-law and a friend—all who had encouraged me. And suddenly even the brook at Cherith dried up (1 Kings 17:7). As a teacher, teaching a crowded class of over sixty for more than four hours a day, six days a week, I tired my voice, and it failed. The doctors diagnosed it as myasthenia laryngitis and said my teaching career was at an end. My world collapsed a second time. My anxiety about the future made my condition worse. Finally, out of sheer desperation, I turned to God.

I thought God had been inconsiderate, and I stormed the gates of heaven. When I had the grace to say, with Daniel, "Yes, I will trust God even if I am not saved" (Dan. 3:17,18), I got back my voice, bit by bit. The Hindu doctor was baffled. Counseling and medicine helped. A Christian neurologist explained that perhaps my disability had been psychosomatic and perhaps my faith had helped me to triumph over it. I finally had the grace to run the next mile, shouting, "I will trust God. Yes, even if I am slain by God's own hands" (Job 13:15).

This experience was perhaps my personal Mount of Transfiguration. For three years, I had lived in limbo, going through the motions of living, with no real verve. Once I learned to trust God absolutely, I was steadily filled with the joy of God's presence. Fears and worries decreased. Circumstances changed. Small promotions came my way. My confidence was restored. I started my theological studies, and God spoke to me in many ways. But the turning point came when my youngest sister literally twisted my arm to speak at a seminar for young widows.

The seminar was called The Widow's Veil. Halfway through recounting my problems, I broke down, and everyone in the audience joined me. But there I met other young widows who were in worse condition. Many were not qualified, not even literate, had no supportive family or friends or any children to live for, and their only means of eking out a living was through selling their flesh. It was then that I began to see God's mission for me—the ministry of reconciliation and encouragement to destitute young women, particularly widows. God taught me first so that I could help and counsel others like me.

I have been a widow for nearly two decades now. During these years God has literally put me through my paces. Now I think I have a grasp of what eternal life is, and that is knowing God and adoring God with love, not for what God can do for me or my loved ones but for what God is. Such a love transcends all earthly conditions and expectations. I love God because God is my friend and my God. And knowing God as God is—that is eternal life. "Now this is eternal life: that they may know you, the only true God" (John 17:3).

As I read God's word and ponder over what it teaches me, different aspects of God are gradually revealed to me, and this peep into divinity and eternal life thrills me and excites my whole being. Then my petty triumphs and losses seem as nothing when "compared to the surpassing greatness of knowing Christ Jesus my Lord" (Phil. 3:8), and because of this, no matter what my status in society is, I celebrate my spirituality jubiliantly.

During these years God has enabled me to establish an operational framework of faith, which I share with other single women. I share some steps of my ladder of faith with the prayer that this may console and strengthen my single sisters; I read somewhere that God has a secret stairway to every heart. I pray that my sisters may find this stairway, meet God halfway, and discover for themselves their spiritual identity.

FAITH TO FIGHT ORTHODOXY

For most young Indian widows, the biggest hurdle is facing the stigma attached to widowhood. So the first step in their rehabilitation is to stop subscribing to the popular fallacies about widowhood. In my own life I had to resolve this before I could take a positive step. This insight came to me when I coordinated the program for young widows. A Scottish pastor and counselor helped me to run a session he could not because many participants did not know English to follow him directly. Under his guidance I ran the session, and it was an eye-opener to me. I put down on the board some fallacies about widows, such as:

1. A widow is accursed of God.
2. A widow is responsible for the death of her husband.
3. A widow is an inauspicious person.

4. A well-dressed, happy widow is asking for trouble.
5. Children of widows are often undisciplined.

Mostly the widows viewed all these as quite correct, without any reservations. It was appalling to me. It is shocking enough that the world around accuses us of being instrumental in our husbands' deaths but it is absolutely self-annihilatory to condemn ourselves.

When I asked the widows why they subscribed to such a view, each had a "valid" reason, according to her. The widow of a well digger had quarreled with him just before he left for work. He never returned home because there was a landslide and he was crushed to death. Another man had taken poison, yet another had drunk illicit liquor, while one was beaten to death. One or two had been terminally ill, and a bus driver was killed in a road accident. Whatever the nature and cause of death, all these widows belived that, directly or indirectly, they had driven their husbands to death. All the widows were heartbroken and none looked like a termagant. Yet all these women accepted that they were accursed, unlucky, and had no right to be other than perpetually mournful.

It is very sad to note that most of these fallacies are perpetuated by women themselves. Though "sati," an old Indian custom of burning the widow along with her husband, is legally prohibited, perhaps that was better than the living death that some widows undergo. In orthodox families the widow cannot participate even in her own daughter's marriage, as she is inauspicious. My family never made me feel inauspicious, but the world outside was not willing to take any risks. I still remember the gasps from my colleagues when my headmistress garlanded me at a felicitation meeting. It was scandalous because as a widow I have no right to wear flowers.

The Indian widow is forbidden many things, such as the wearing of nose and toe rings, keeping the saffron bhindhi on the forehead, applying turmeric paste while bathing, being smartly dressed. Rebelliousness and perhaps my own conceit did not allow me to conform to the mournful appearance befitting a widow. As a Christian, whether married or widowed, I never longed for these outward symbols of my married status because these are the Hindu marks of auspiciousnes. But God has given me a cheerful nature, and I love to dress well and to carry myself with confidence—not with the expected self-effacement. For this I am often criticized, and sometimes it hurts.

Then I met an old lady who was widowed in her sixteenth year, about 1912. Life must have been even more terrible for her in those days. She explained to me Hosea 2:15 in the light of her experience. My widowhood is the valley of Achor—the valley of troubles and a symbol of shame. But God offers to transform my valley of Achor into a Door of Hope. She convinced me that I am not an accursed being but one chosen by God to be espoused to God forever, that I am betrothed to God forever (Hos. 2:16, 19–20, 18, 54). This lady's witness and her exposition of the Bible verses helped me to reject totally all the myths about widowhood and to look upon widowhood as a Door of Hope. With God beside me, I was to explore the opportunities open to me and to flourish.

God reminded me of a favorite verse of mine—I Peter 2:9. As a child I had praised God for my Christian faith which has liberated me from the many narrow-minded, inhibiting, and superstitious customs that even my Hindu first cousins are bound by. Now this verse shone through the darkness of my misery. It showed me clearly that even if some Indian Christians subscribe to the views of our natives about widowhood, the blood of Christ has set me free from these. It is now up to me to appropriate this liberation. Therefore I believe I am not an accursed person but I am God's chosen one, heir to glory and of the royal household of Christ. So with Paul in Romans 8:35–39 I say, "Who shall separate me from the love of Christ? Shall widowhood, death, trouble, or hardship or persecution? No. In all these things we are more than conquerors. Neither death nor life . . . will be able to separate us from the Love of God."

Then God revealed to me other aspects of my name "Beulah-married" and, by extension, "fruitful." I have come to believe first that God named me Beulah not because he wants me to be auspicious for myself but that I might be fruitful for others. "Beulah-land" is a heaven that enjoys God's presence always. Second, I must be a haven for other shipwrecked sisters while they repair their shattered souls. Third, I realize that I was not married in the sense of being married for years, a situation in which many couples forget the magic of their early love, but in the sense of being an eager bride, waiting with joy and hope for that day of God's coming, for "now I know in part; then I shall know fully, even as I am fully known" (1 Cor. 13:12b).

This conviction makes it possible for me to celebrate my spirituality. Thanks be to Christ who has made me realize my own worth, for He loved me unto death and I am precious to Him. Because I am his bride, joint heiress, and of the royal priesthood, I shall rejoice and sing for joy. I shall smile and dress impeccably, as my body is his temple.

I shall walk cheerfully but circumspectly—not as the world would want me to but as my Leader whose bride I am would expect of me, and I take care not to sully God's Holy name. And I shall not be cowed by oppressive orthodoxy, for God, who is mightier than orthodoxy, has done great things for me. Therefore "my soul glorifies and my spirit rejoices in God my savior" (Luke 1:45, 47).

FAITH TO PERCEIVE THE FENCE OF SECURITY

The next step in the framework of my spirituality is the firm conviction that I am in the protective circle of God. A young widow in an androcentric society is in a very vulnerable position. She is the prime target for all kinds of exploitation. The worst and the most humiliating kind is that of sexual harassment by lecherous men. To me this has been and still is a major problem and a threat to my peace of mind.

I have been the recipient of the most dishonorable propositions, and I know other widows who have needed great diplomacy and skill in warding off such propositions without denting the egos of such men. These men unfortunately happen to be colleagues or bosses. In a country where the unemployment rate is high, a widow with a family to support cannot jeopardize her job, and some men take advantage of this state of affairs.

There are of course many gallant men who help without any base ulterior motive, men of the calibre of the biblical Boaz, who helped Ruth with a pure heart. In fact, it required careful orchestration by Ruth's mother-in-law to get Boaz to propose to Ruth. But such mothers-in-law are a very rare breed. Remarriage is one remedy, but a widow with a family gets proposals that are tantamount to jumping from the frying pan into the fire. The majority of men who offer to remarry are either widowers or divorcés with families of their own. This is not bad in itself, but some of them want the widow to forget her past, her relatives, even her own children and belong exclusively to the new family.

Let me illustrate with a proposal brought by one pastor for his colleague, who wanted me to leave my daughter with my aged parents, stay with his family while he went abroad for his master's in theology, and look after his parents and sisters with my salary. The worst of it was that I was to come with all my jewels! What was in it for me? Separation from my daughter and slavery to another inconsiderate family? I asked the pastor's wife why I should yield to such a proposal, and she immediately responded that the proposing pastor was generous enough to marry a widow. Even now I bristle at their audacity. I told her that I was not desperate for a man.

Other similar proposals come from almost senile men or those impotent or severely handicapped. At least these are honest proposals, and for some widows they promise security. The most insulting proposals come from men who are "happily married" but want a mistress to pander to their ego. In their conceit they cannot accept a curt no from the single woman. They think she is playing hard to get and can be won over by and by or they label the woman as frigid or even bring false charges about her work and conduct.

Stereotypes can be dangerous, but the following is the stereotype of such men, based on the experiences of many single women: these men are in positions of power—often as boss or a superior—are married with a family, are often past middle age but trying to look younger, dress smartly, take tonics and tablets that are supposed to rejuvenate them, and are generally very conscious of how they look.

Their modus operandi is very subtle. Their propositions are highly ambiguous. They praise the single woman for her courage, looks, and intelligence and groan about how incompatible their wives are, how they are unloving and frigid or indifferent and certainly not very intelligent. They say what a boon the single woman is, how much joy she could bring into both their lives if she would very discreetly cooperate. They woo her with gifts, often extravagant and totally dispensable ones. Some women who have a low self-image or a battered ego fall easy victims.

Some single women who refuse are branded as frigid. Others live in daily trepidation, and much of their energy is spent in outsmarting such men while retaining their dignity and honor. A widow faces a double jeopardy if she has a young daughter. Even though such men exist, India is basically a moralistic country, and nobody wants to have any association with a woman with a bad reputation or of doubtful conduct. My daughter will be branded forever if I do not preserve my reputation. The widow cannot tell the world that she is blameless, because people are not willing to give her even the benefit of the doubt. So most single women endure without sharing their problems with anyone.

Even if she shared her problems, the double standards in the male-dominated society will not let others listen to the widow objectively. In our society a widower ought to remarry and preferably within a year, but if a widow does, she is considered immoral. Similarly in the harassment issues: the male is sheltered by his marriage, his own wife will be his staunchest defender, and society will say the single woman was the serpent in the garden of his married life.

Can I celebrate my spirituality when I cannot expect justice or even a fair hearing? Yes, I can and I do. The only thing that is left for me is to gird up my loins and fight the good fight. God says, "He that touches you touches the apple of my eye." God's promises for the widow are many. Because I am God's bride, I am not tempted by shoddy proposals. I have seen God act and intervene when I stay within the protective circle. I can cite any number of experiences: from the jaws of the lion, the bear, and even from the horns of rhinoceros, I have been delivered. The trap snapped and I could fly away (Psalms 21, 124:7).

God gives me the courage to be the female counterpart of Joseph in the house of Potiphar, and I dare to defy. Once when I was pressured to stay on at an office after everybody had left to wait for the boss, whose intentions were questionable, I heard God's voice. I was asked if I was going to be another Lot's wife, lingering behind for fear of spoiling my chances for promotion. That was enough; I fled as if all the devils were after me.

It is God who vindicates (Isa. 54:14–17). I feel sorry that the vindication is not instantaneous so that the world might realize that we have a mighty savior to fight our battles, but God waits for an opportune moment and is never late even by a fraction of a second. Let me tell you an incident.

One boss whom I had offended by not yielding turned the tables on me. He said I was impertinent and quoted "Hell hath no fury like a woman scorned." My colleagues knew the truth, but as he was a vindictive person they did not question him but goaded me to complain to the board. They had their own axes to grind. I chose to be transferred. Later he was charged with misappropriation and before action could be taken against him, he died due to a massive heart attack. Many said it was just punishment, but I pity his innocent wife, who has to suffer now.

A year later I found another verse to use when I reach the end of my tether. It reads thus:

You shall not afflict any widow or orphan. If you do afflict them and they cry out to me, I will surely hear their cry: and my wrath will burn and I will kill you with the sword, and your wives shall become widows and your children fatherless. (Exod. 22: 22–24)

This verse has given me tremendous strength, not because I can cry to God to eliminate my enemy, because certainly I do not want the wife or the children of a wicked man to suffer, and I pray I will never be driven to use this promise against anyone. Nevertheless, my heart overflows with adoration for a God who cares so much for my well-being. Every time I read this verse, I can feel the Presence of God, ever vigilant to rush to my defense.

I can tell you of many incidents in the lives of many sisters when God was like a wall of fire about them, vindicating them before the eyes of the world. I know from my own personal experience that it is God who justifies me and protects me. Therefore, I have reason to celebrate; there is no other God who can deliver so wonderfully.

FAITH TO PERSEVERE

In spite of my Christian conviction, I have often wondered if life is worth living. Why do I put up with all my groaning and anguish? Does anyone care what happens to me?

Will I ever see a bright, peaceful future? Sometimes life's major problems seem easier to tackle than the daily pinpricks of life. But my faith reasserts itself. God will restore unto me the years the locusts have eaten. Like Job I will get back whatever I have lost with compensation—not in some distant future but here in the land of the living (Psalm 27:13), and this helps me to persevere against odds. I cannot give up, because God promises to sustain me through everything.

In addition, I have to forge ahead to give my daughter a secure life, because if life is difficult for a widow, it is almost unendurable for the orphan, particularly for the girl child. So I took stock of my assets. I read about the widow who approached Elisha to help her pay off her husband's creditors. He asked her, "Tell me, what do you have in your house?" (2 Kings 4:2). She had only a little oil. He then helped her to multiply her only asset and to pay off her debts. This incident challenged me, and while thinking about it, I joined a theological course. There God showed me that I have the ability to study.

I asked my heavenly Elisha to help me invest this, my only talent and he did, far beyond my wildest dreams. My increased qualification brought me higher pay and also opened up other income-generating avenues. This means that at times I combine two or three different activities that provide the jam for our bread and butter. This also means that I work very hard, forego most of the pleasures, and work during vacations, but I thank God who has made me financially independent. I thank God, who sends many opportunities my way and who empowers me to work (Deut. 8:184). Since the extra work I do is seasonal, I live day by day on faith, as when I went to study without any pay.

For twenty years, God has provided my daily manna. My groceries stretch. The flour and the oil have never run out. My clothes wear well. The only thing that I wear out fast are my slippers. This may be because I do not work enough as an evangelist, whose feet are beautiful on the mountains (Isa. 52:7). But I do appropriate for my daughter and myself all the special provisions God has made for the widow and her child (Deut. 24:19–21, 26:12,13, 27:19). My colleagues and friends often say that God has done great things for me, and I tell myself that they cannot fully know how much has been done for me.

I do have my share of anxious moments, mainly due to my poor faith. I become nervous, short-tempered, and quarrelsome and get ruffled easily. Then I see that by losing my equanimity, I conform myself to the world's standard for single women of my circumstances, for example, being hysterical, flighty, indecisive, and even neurotic. I also realize that I disappoint God by not making use of the resources available, by not claiming God's peace, power, and wisdom. So I pray for poise and serenity, an unflappability that can only come from the unassailable conviction that God is in control and all I have to do is yield everything, even my flickering faith, and God shall do everything else for me.

I shall rejoice and celebrate my spirituality. I hear God's clarion call.

Bibliography

Anthony, Katharine. *Susan B. Anthony: Her Personal History and Her Era.* New York: Doubleday, 1954.

Bakan, David. *The Duality of Human Existence: An Essay on Psychology and Religion.* Chicago: Rand McNally, 1966.

Bakos, Susan Crain. *This Wasn't Supposed to Happen: Single Women Over Thirty Talk Frankly about Their Lives.* New York: Continuum, 1985.

Brown, Gabrielle. *The New Celibacy.* New York: McGraw-Hill, 1980.

Boff, Leonardo. *El Rostro Materno de Dios.* Translated by Alfonso Ortiz. Madrid: Ediciones Biblicas Paulinas, 1979.

Campbell, Joseph. *The Power of Myth.* New York: Doubleday, 1988.

Cassidy, Sheila. *Audacity to Believe.* London: Darton, Longman and Todd, 1992.

———. *Good Friday People.* London: Darton, Longman and Todd, 1991.

———. *Sharing the Darkness.* London: Darton, Longman and Todd, 1989.

Clarkson, Margaret. *So You're Single!* Wheaton, Ill.: Harold Shaw Publishers, 1979.

Cohen, Leah. *Small Expectations.* Toronto: McLelland & Stewart, 1984.

Craighead, Meinrad. "Meinrad Craighead." In Anne Bancroft, ed., *Weavers of Wisdom: Women Mystics of the Twentieth Century.* London: Arkana, 1989.

Daly, Mary. *Beyond God the Father.* Boston: Beacon Press, 1973.

Dillard, Annie. *Pilgrim at Tinker Creek.* New York: Harper's Magazine Press, 1974.

Downey, Michael. *A Blessed Weakness: The Spirit of Jean Vanier and L'Arche.* San Francisco: Harper & Row, 1986.

Doyle, Brendan. *Meditations with Julian of Norwich.* Sante Fe, N.M.: Bear and Company, 1983.

Duin, Julia. *Purity Makes the Heart Grow Stronger: Sexuality and the Single Christian.* Ann Arbor, Mich.: Servant Books, 1988.

Eagly, Alice. *Sex Differences in Social Behavior: A Social-Role Interpretation.* Hillsdale, N.J.: Erlbaum, 1987.

Eagly, Alice H., and Steffen, Valerie J. "Gender Stereotypes Stem from the Distribution of Women and Men into Social Roles." *Journal of Personality and Social Psychology* 46 (April 1984): 735–754.

Etaugh, Claire, and Petroski, Barbara. "Perceptions of Women: Effects of Employment Status and Marital Status." *Sex Roles* 12 (February 1985): 329–339.

Fracchia, Charles A. *Living Alone Together: The New American Monasticism.* San Francisco: Harper & Row, 1979.

Gigy, Lynn L. "Self-Concept of Single Women." *Psychology of Women Quarterly* 5 (Winter 1980): 321–340.

Gove, Walter R. "The Relationship between Sex Roles, Marital Status, and Mental Illness." *Social Forces* 51 (September 1972): 34–44.

Griffith, Gwyneth. "Images of Interdependence: Meaning and Movement in Learning/Teaching." Ed.D. dissertation, University of Toronto, 1982.

Groeschel, Benedict J. *The Courage to Be Chaste.* New York: Paulist Press, 1985.

Haney, Eleanor H. *Vision and Struggle: Meditations on Feminist Spirituality and Politics.* Portland: Astarte Shell Press, 1989.

Hares, Betty. *Journeying into Openness.* Bristol, England: Shoreline, 1991.

Harris, Maria. *Dance of the Spirit: The Seven Steps of Women's Spirituality.* New York: Bantam, 1989.

Heschel, Abraham Joshua. *The Sabbath, Its Meaning for Modern Man.* New York: Farrar, Straus and Giroux, 1951.

Holdsworth, Christopher. University of Exeter, Degree Orations, July 1991.

Hughes, Rev. Selwyn. *Every Day with Jesus.* Surrey, England: CWR Publication, 1984.

Hunt, Mary E. *Fierce Tenderness: A Feminist Theology of Friendship.* New York: Crossroad, 1991.

Illich, Ivan. *Celebration of Awareness.* Harmondsworth, Middlesex, Great Britain: Penguin, 1973.

———. *Deschooling Society.* Harmondsworth, Middlesex, Great Britain: Penguin, 1973.

———. *Limits to Medicine.* Harmondsworth, Middlesex, Great Britain: Pelican, 1977.

———. *Tools for Conviviality.* New York: Harper & Row, 1973.

Israel, Martin. *Living Alone: The Spiritual Dimension.* New York: Crossroad, 1983.

Jones, W. Paul. *The Province across the River.* Nashville, Tenn.: The Upper Room, 1986.

Kazantzakis, Nikos. *Zorba the Greek.* New York: Ballantine, 1965.

Kelly, Thomas. *A Testament of Devotion.* New York: Harper & Row, 1941.

Lyndon Baines Johnson Presidential Library. Lady Bird Johnson Room. Austin, Texas.

Lyon, William. *A Pew for One, Please.* New York: Crossroad, 1977.

McFague, Sallie. *Metaphorical Theology: Models of God in Religious Language.* Philadelphia: Fortress Press, 1982.

McLaughlin, Eleanor, and Ruether, Rosemary Radford, editors. *Women of Spirit: Female Leadership in the Jewish and Christian Traditions.* New York: Simon & Schuster, 1979.

Moustakas, Clark E. *Loneliness.* Englewood Cliffs, N.J.: Prentice Hall, 1961.

————. *Loneliness and Love.* Englewood Cliffs, N.J.: Prentice Hall, 1972.

Muto, Susan Annette. *Blessings that Make Us Be: A Formative Approach to Living the Beatitudes.* Petersham, Mass.: St. Bede's Publications, 1990.

————. *Celebrating the Single Life: A Spirituality for Single Persons in Today's World.* New York: Crossroad, 1989.

————. "Family, Friendship and the Single Life." *The Family* (October 1988): 28–30.

————. "Loving Family Members while Living Singly." *The Family* (November 1988): 4–5.

————. *Pathways of Spiritual Living.* Petersham, Mass.: St. Bede's Publications, 1988.

Muto, Susan Annette, and van Kaam, Adrian. *Commitment: Key to Christian Maturity.* New York: Paulist Press, 1989.

National Women's Hall of Fame. Elizabeth Cady Stanton Exhibit. Seneca Falls, N.Y.

Pascal, Blaise. *Pensées.* New York: Viking Penguin, 1966.

"Planning for Single Young Adult Ministry: Directions for Ministerial Outreach." Department of Education, United States Catholic Conference, 1981.

Riso, Don Richard. *Personality Types.* Boston: Houghton Mifflin, 1987.

Ritter, Erika. *Urban Scrawl.* Toronto: Macmillan of Canada, 1984.

Roosevelt, Anna Eleanor. *The Autobiography of Eleanor Roosevelt.* New York: Harper & Brothers, 1961.

Ruether, Rosemary Radford. *Women-Church: Theology and Practice of Feminist Liturgical Communities.* San Francisco: Harper & Row, 1986.

Saint-Exupéry, Antoine de. *The Little Prince.* Translated by Katherine Woods. New York: Harcourt Brace & World, 1943.

Sarton, May. *At Seventy: A Journal.* New York: Norton, 1987.

————. *Journal of a Solitude.* New York: Norton, 1973.

————. *Letters from Maine: New Poems.* New York: Norton, 1984.

————. *Recovering: A Journal.* New York: Norton, 1980.

————. "Wilderness Lost." In *The Silence Now.* New York: Norton, 1988.

Schaef, Anne Wilson. *Escape from Intimacy: Untangling the "Love" Addictions: Sex, Romance, Relationships.* New York: Harper & Row, 1989.

————. *Women's Reality: An Emerging Female System in a White Male Society.* New York: Harper & Row, 1985.

Seabrook, Jeremy. *Loneliness.* New York: Universe, 1973.

Steindl-Rast, David. *Gratefulness, the Heart of Prayer: An Approach to Life in Fullness*. New York: Paulist Press, 1984.

Storr, Anthony. *Solitude*. London: Fontana Paperbacks, 1988.

Tileston, Mary Wilder, editor. *Joy & Strength*. Minneapolis: World Wide Publications, 1986. Original imprint, 1901.

Van de Kemp, Hendrika, and Schreck, G. Peter. "The Church's Ministry to Singles: A Family Model." *Journal of Religion and Health* 20, no. 2 (Summer 1981): 141-155.

van Kaam, Adrian. *Spirituality and the Gentle Life*. Denville, N.J.: Dimension, 1974.

_____ . *Women at the Well*. Denville, N.J.: Dimension, 1976.

Vanier, Jean. *Community and Growth*. London: Darton, Longman and Todd, 1989.

Voillaume, Rene. *Seeds of the Desert: The Legacy of Charles de Foucauld*. Wheathampstead, Hertfordshire, Great Britain: Anthony Clarke, 1972.

Williams H. A. *Tensions*. London: Mitchell Beazley, 1976.

Wiltsher, Anne. *Most Dangerous Women: Feminist Peace Campaigners of the Great War*. London: Pandora Press, 1985.

Winter, Miriam Therese. *Woman Prayer, Woman Song: Resources for Ritual*. Oak Park, N.Y.: Meyer Stone Books, 1987.

Woolf, Virginia. *A Room of One's Own*. London: Hogarth Press, 1929.

A Woman's Notebook III: Being a Blank Book with Quotes by Women. Philadelphia: Running Press, 1983.

Index

About the Editors and Contributors

MARY O'BRIEN is in the Gerontology and Women's Studies Departments at Mount St. Vincent University in Halifax, Nova Scotia, Canada. She is also Director of the Nova Scotia Centre on Aging. She has done research on older ever-single women and on women, work, and the cost of care giving to the elderly. She is presently involved in research exploring spirituality with older women and analyzing their perceptions of the meaning of spirituality and spiritual development over the life cycle.

CLARE CHRISTIE is an ever-single in her midforties. An educator for twelve years, for some time now she has been a lawyer with Kenneth A. MacInnis Associates in Halifax, Nova Scotia, Canada. Her main areas of practice are "little-people law": family, wills and estates, and property. Volunteer activities combine her interests in justice, feminism, peace, spirituality, and the intellectually challenged. Leisure pastimes include family and friends, outdoor activities, reading, writing, and gardening at her century-old city and shore properties.

ALICE BRONA is a mother and mystic and a former public health nurse. She is an associate of Holy Cross Centre for Ecology and Spirituality in Port Burwell, Ontario, Canada.

ESLY REGINA CARVALHO, Brazilian-born psychotherapist, heads the Ministries to the Family, Women and Children for the Latin American Council of Churches in La Paz, Bolivia.

SHEILA CASSIDY is an ever-single, a doctor, and a writer. She is medical director of a hospice for the terminally ill in Great Britain and has lectured widely on care for the dying.

MARY ANN CEJKA is an ever-single doctoral student in social psychology at Purdue University, Indiana. She has offered workshops and written on women in the church.

LIN COLLETTE is a divorced doctoral student in American Religious Studies at the Union Institute, Cincinnati, Ohio, studying extreme right Christian groups.

E. MARGARET FULTON, past president of Mount Saint Vincent University, has received, in addition to three earned degrees, many honorary degrees and awards of distinction, including the Order of Canada. As teacher, professor, and administrator, she has experienced the difficulties encountered by single women in a patriarchal society.

GWYNETH GRIFFITH, now a free-lance educational consultant, has worked in child welfare and for the YWCA. She is an active laywoman in the United Church of Canada.

GLORIA W. GROVER is a divorced grandmother, a writer, and a pensioner living in Vancouver, British Columbia, Canada.

BETTY HARES was a missionary in China and Ghana, Executive Secretary of the Methodist Missionary Society, and editor of NOW. She teaches theology students, writes, and paints.

JO ELLEN HEIL is a free-lance writer, researcher, and lecturer in Women's Herstory. She is ever-single and works in a children's bookstore in Ventura, California.

BEVERLEY HOLT, ever-single, is a spiritual director who was formerly National Baptist Youth Director for the Baptist Union of New Zealand.

BEULAH JEYASEELI is a widow and mother and a member of the Tamil Evangelical Lutheran Church. She is headmistress of a girls' Christian school in Tamil Nadu, India.

LILA LINE has published many articles and two books. She teaches writing classes at Chesapeake College, Maryland, and is a photographer. She is divorced.

PAMELA ANN MOELLER, an ordained minister, is Assistant Professor of Public Worship at Emmanuel College, Victoria University, in Toronto, Ontario, Canada. She is divorced.

VICKI MORGAN is an ever-single Quaker who describes herself as a "generalist at large." She is currently working in a small bookstore in Portland, Oregon.

MABEL A. MURRAY was for thirty-four years in religious life. She began a Waldorf School in Idaho and is presently principal of a small Roman Catholic school in West Virginia.

SUSAN MUTO is executive director of the Epiphany Association in Pittsburgh, Pennsylvania.

EILEEN E. O'BRIEN is the systems administrator of the Los Angeles Archdiocese in California. She is working on an M.A. in Religious Studies at Mount Saint Mary's College, Los Angeles.

TRICIA OGISTE was born in the Caribbean and moved as an adult to Toronto, Ontario, Canada. She is ever-single and a devout Roman Catholic.

ROBERTA WAY-CLARK is a widow, a writer and broadcaster specializing in seniors, and was first director of the Care for the Caregiver program in Halifax, Nova Scotia, Canada.